Dedicated to the memory of Mandy Lifeboats
without whom none of this would have happened.

She was alright, our Mnads!!

Collated and Produced by Edina Cloud and Kelly Sigh

Published by Charity Goods in 2008 ©

This book has been created and published in aid
of BBC Children in Need.

No part of this publication may be reproduced or transmitted in any form or by any means electric or mechanical, nor may it be stored in any retrieval system without prior permission from the publisher.

Charity Goods © 2008

TOGS would like to thank ESP Colour, with their help in printing this brochure

FOREWORD

TOGS could just as easily be known as TOTS, Terry's Old Trenchermen and Women. The buffet table at the yearly TOGS Convention has skin and hair flying in all directions, not to mention fish fingers, quiche and chipolatas. One mustn't carp or cavil, however, for they only follow in the proud tradition of "Wake Wogan Up"(Monday to Saturday, 7 to 9am, BBC Light Programme) of which they claim to be faithful followers, but, in fact, only use as a front, or excuse, for aliases, double entendres, and not acting their age.

Look, if I'm known for anything, it's my racing snake physique. I eat but frugally, but am sadly surrounded by underlings and hangers-on, who eat and drink like savages, and whose daily whine is for victuals and provender.

These shameless gormandisers put themselves outside a constant stream of snorkers, pies, fish and chips, full English, curries and turkey at Christmas. When I mildly rebuke these peons, fastidiously averting my eyes from their excesses, they answer back: "We've been up since 5 this morning! It's lunchtime for us!"

This slim volume is a desperate attempt by some right-thinking TOGS to redress the balance, to substitute fine (or "Top-End") dining in place of the shameless gorging that has been going on in my name. In the immortal words of Masterchef's ingredients expert, what you'll get here is "A nice plate of food!"

TOGS tickle your palate....

Terry Wogan.

Knowing how much Togs like food (and drink!) a Tog named Mandy Lifeboats had a brilliant idea in 2000 - a Togs Cookbook in aid of Children In Need. She collected a variety of recipes from a wide range of sources and produced a very successful tome. She always intended that there would be a second volume and discussed the possibility with Hellen Bach, but before she could undertake this new project Mandy became ill and sadly we lost her to cancer in 2007.

So when Hellen decided the time was right for the next book I was honoured to be asked to collate the contributions from Togs and the Radio 2 personalities.

And here it is - the Togs Cookbook Volume 2. By buying this book you are not only developing your range of culinary skills and maybe trying out dishes that are new to you, you are also contributing to this very worthy charity.

Just as Togs take no notice of use-by dates, many of these recipes show they feel the same about weighing and measuring. * Some have used grams and litres, but then again we still have lbs and ozs, and even "cups" in some cases. I have kept to the original measurements sent in, as presumably they are tried and tested and therefore work, so you will find a mixture of metric and imperial.

Thank you to everyone who has provided recipes to enable this book to be produced, and special thanks to the Togmeister himself, Sir Terry Wogan, the inspiration to us all.

Warning - Each reader is responsible for their own food consumption (I'm not getting caught out by the "health and safety" brigade)!!

Edina Cloud

*Editor's Note – what, no scales, Edi?

BUTTERNUT SQUASH SOUP

This soup is not only delicious it makes great comfort food. One day, visiting my American priest friend, Gail, during a difficult time in my life, she served up this soup. It was heaven sent!

Ingredients:

Butternut squash	Butter
3 Tbsp brown sugar	2 Tbsp maple syrup
3 cups chicken stock	2 Tbsp dry Sherry*
½ tspn ground cumin	½ - 1 cup double cream
Salt and pepper to taste	

Method:

- Peel and de-seed a butternut squash.
- Cut it into roast-potato-size pieces and place in a baking tray with about 1cm or more of water in the bottom. Dot with butter.
- Shake over brown sugar and maple syrup
- Roast at 200 C in a fan oven until cooked.
- Puree the squash with the liquor in the tray.
- Add the chicken stock, Sherry, cream and cumin and salt and pepper.

You may need to add more stock or sherry and you can add 1 tbs more of maple syrup and 2tbs more of brown sugar, but I don't find it needs anymore of the sweet ingredients usually.

Serve hot with a dollop of Crème Fraiche in it, and a hunk of Walnut Bread on the side. I'm dribbling at the thought!

*I add about half a cup!

Rev Ruth Scott
Top Ecclesiastical Totty

HOKY POKY NETTLE SOUP
(Have some dock leaves handy)

Ingredients:

- 2-3 stinging nettle tops (ouch)
- 4 Tbsp single cream
- 1 oz butter
- 4 oz onion finely chopped
- Pinch of salt
- Thinly sliced lemon
- 8 oz potatoes peeled and coarsely chopped
- 1½ pints of chicken stock or 2 stock cubes and water

Method:

- Wash and drain nettles
- Slowly cook onions and potatoes in melted butter for about 5 mins (do not brown)
- Add salt and stock and bring to boil.
- Add nettles and return to the boil then reduce heat.
- Simmer for about 30 mins till potatoes are tender.
- Liquidise and return soup to pan and bring to the boil again
- Turn off the heat and when a little cooler stir in the cream, pepper and more salt.
- Serve with thin slices of lemon floating on top.

(it doesnt sting when cooked !)

Jilly Oxborrow of Sunny Scunny

MINESTRONE SOUP

Ingredients:

1 leek	1 large tin tomatoes
1 onion	1 level tsp basil
1 carrot	1 level tsp salt
2 sticks celery	1 level tsp sugar
150g white or green cabbage	800ml water
1 small pkt frozen green beans	50g macaroni
50g haricot beans (soaked overnight)	
2 level tbsp finely chopped parsley	

Method:

- Trim leek and cut in half lengthwise. Wash thoroughly under cold running water.
- Wash celery and cabbage and peel onion and carrot.
- Chop all 5 vegetables finely.
- Place prepared vegetables in large pan.
- Drain soaking liquid from haricot beans.
- Add rest of ingredients EXCEPT MACARONI to pan.
- Bring to the boil, lower heat and cover pan.
- Simmer gently for 1 hour.
- Add macaroni and simmer another 15 minutes until pasta is soft.

Edina Cloud

DAVID JACOBS' FAVOURITE SOUP HOT OR COLD
MADE BY HIS WIFE LINDSAY

Serves 6

Ingredients:

- 1 bunch of spring onions chopped
- 2oz butter
- 2 slices of good thick cut ham
- 1 lettuce heart torn
- Big packet of frozen peas
- 1 tablespoon caster sugar
- Good handful of fresh mint chopped
- salt and black pepper
- 2 pints chicken stock plus one organic stock cube

Double cream ⎫
Croutons   ⎬ To serve
            ⎭

Method:

- Gently saute the onions in a little butter until tender.
- Add all the ingredients (not the cream or croutons!) to the pan and simmer for 30mins.
- Blend in the liquidiser until fairly smooth
  We like it quite thick but if you prefer it thinner just add some more stock.

We have it with a swirl of cream and croutons cut with a heart shape cutter. Just fry in a little butter and put more in a small bowl to pass round.

Lovely cold but also great warm on Boxing Day with star shaped croutons.

David Jacobs

PEA POD SOUP

Ingredients:

Large handful of peapods	Water to cover
Cream to taste	2 onions
Small piece of leek	Large potato
Small piece of ginger	Small piece of chilli
Fresh mint, handful	Salt, pepper

Mixed fresh herbs, little of each if possible….fennel herb, chives, oregano, parsley

Method:

- Leave pods whole, chop onion, potato, leek, ginger and chilli, chop or bruise the mint
- Put all the ingredients except the cream into a pan and bring to the boil
- Take out pods, keep a few for garnish, plus a mint leaf
- Add the cream and whizz in blender
- Serve and eat, beautiful subtle minty pea flavour

Graham Dunbar

DEBBIE'S SWEET POTATO, COCONUT & LIME SOUP

Ingredients:

- 1 large white onion (or 2 smaller ones)
- 1 large or 2 medium Sweet Potatoes (app. 750-900g / 1.5-2lb)
- 1 tin of Coconut Milk (we use the lower fat / lighter one) 440g
- 1 ltr of chicken or vegetable stock (go for veg if you're going to serve it to non meat-eaters)
- 1 tsp Green Thai Paste
- 1 Lime

Method:

- Peel and top and tail your onions. Then slice or chop - it doesn't matter which, you're going to blend them later.
- Put into a large saucepan, just cover with boiled water and set on the heat to sweat - you don't want them crispy, just translucent.
- Peel your potatoes and dice into 1.5cm cubes (that's half an inch near as dammit for those of you that work in old money!)
- Boil the kettle. Mix your stock in a jug, using the boiled water - ensure well dissolved. If your stock is already liquid, don't add any more water!
- Once the onions are nicely sweated - add to the pan your sweet potato cubes, coconut milk, stock, and green thai paste - then squeeze in the juice of your lime.
- Pop a lid on the pan, bring to the boil, then simmer for 20 minutes or so - until the potato is soft.
- Allow to cool slightly, then blend to a thick creamy consistency. If it's too gloopy, add a little more stock.

Makes app. 1.5ltrs so enough to serve 6 easily. Is also very good as a base for curries.

Debbie Lee

HONEYMOON SALAD

Lettuce alone !

(One iceberg lettuce, washed and shredded. Garnish to taste)

Linda Murrell

JANICE LONG'S SAVOURY SPECIAL

Hope this will fit the bill.... this is a favourite in our house...

Ingredients:

    Halloumi, diced   Crushed red chilli

    Spinach   Sunflower and / or pumpkin seeds

    Rye bread, toasted

Method:

Dry fry some diced halloumi until slightly brown, chuck in some crushed red chilli, add a load of spinach leaves and let them wilt. Add sunflower, pumpkin seeds etc. and serve on toasted rye bread. Pour on a little dressing made up of olive oil, balsamic vinegar, lemon juice and crushed garlic. Can also add rocket, sweet pepper, and fresh beetroot. Heaven! I am salivating as I write.

JANICE LONG

ENGLISH BREAKFAST STARTER

This does what it says on the tin!
All the ingredients of a full English breakfast, but served as a starter. This is a good dinner party recipe as it can largely be prepared in advance and served cold.

Ingredients:

- Bread
- Egg mayonnaise
- Ham
- Chorizo (or similar) sausage
- Black pudding
- Tomato, sliced

Method:

- Use a pastry cutter or glass about the same size as the black pudding to cut the bread and the ham into circles.

- Fry a chopped up rasher of bacon in the pan first for flavour, then just fry the black pudding lightly before frying the bread until it's crispy and golden brown.

- Once cooked pat the croutons and black pudding dry with some kitchen towel to remove any excess fat.

- Make a stack comprising of a fried bread crouton, black pudding, a slice of ham, Chorizo (or similar) sausage, another slice of ham and a slice of tomato topped with chopped boiled egg and mayonnaise.

- Serve with a green leaf salad.

Glen B Ogle

STUFFED TOMATOES

Ingredients:

2 beef tomatoes	1 tbsp extra virgin olive oil
1 small onion	125g Mozzarella cheese
1 clove garlic, optional	1 egg, beaten
1 tspn dried oregano	2 tbsp Parmesan cheese
30g breadcrumbs, wholemeal or white	

Method:

- Halve the tomatoes widthways and scoop out middle.
- Peel and chop onion and garlic.
- Heat olive oil in small pan and cook onion and garlic for few minutes until soft.
- Mix together onion, garlic, breadcrumbs, oregano, Parmesan and beaten egg.
- Drain Mozzarella and cut into 8 slices.
- Place the 4 smaller pieces in the hollowed out tomato halves.
- Fill tomatoes with breadcrumb mixture and top each with remaining Mozzarella slices.
- Place in ovenproof dish and bake at Gas 5 or 190C for approximately 15 minutes or until cheese is melted and tomatoes are cooked.
- ** Can be used as starter or main course.

Har Monica

SMOKED MACKEREL PATE

Ingredients:

- 2 x large peppered smoked mackerel fillets, skinned
- 4 oz. half fat cottage cheese
- 5 oz 0% Fat Greek yoghurt
- Juice of a lemon
- 1 chopped spring onion
- Grated nutmeg, mace, cayenne and black pepper (to taste – probably about half a teaspoon of the mixed spices)

Method:

Mash all the ingredients together with a fork until smoothish. Serve with toast or crispbread. Serves 4 – 5

CHEESE PATE

Ingredients:

- 1lb cream cheese
- 1lb Red Leics cheese, grated
- ½ small green pepper, chopped
- ½ small red pepper, chopped
- 2 – 3 spring onions, chopped
- Freshly ground black pepper
- 4oz melted butter

Method:

Mash the cream cheese with the grated Red Leicester and mix in all the other ingredients. Fill a 2lb loaf tin and press down. Chill. Turn out by dipping in hot water and running a hot knife around the edge. Serve with thinly sliced toast or with crusty bread.

This is "party" quantities. If you do not wish to use a 2lb tin, you can put into individual portions and freeze for when you want them.

Carol Dickens

CHEESEY EGGS

I always associate good food with great friends.

Whenever I dropped in on my friend, Joan, she was always up to her elbows in gardening, but after a quick scrub-up she'd line two ramekin dishes with cheddar cheese, break an egg into each, fill the ramekin dishes to the top with single or double cream, sprinkle them with curry powder and put them on a baking tray to bake in her Aga for about 15 minutes (about 160 degrees centigrade)

Served straight from the oven with a hunk of bread, they're delicious. And so easy! They make a great starter for a dinner party.

Rev Ruth Scott
Top Ecclesiastical Totty

RECIPE FOR DISASTER

Take a rare Welsh bit from Splot

Add Barralands to the cooking pot

Throw in Boggy, Nove and Fran

And Deadly (quite a tasty man)

Garnish it with Tel the Master

And you've a recipe for disaster!

Jilly Oxborrow of Sunny Scunny

BRUNTONSIDE'S STRATHDON BLUE CHEESE BRULÉE

This was a recipe that I pinched from a South African friend who used Roquefort. To give it a Scottish slant, I experimented with a few blues before settling for Ruaraidh Stone's rich & creamy Strathdon blue.

Serve on a plate decorated with flashes of pear & saffron compote and little blue cheese biscuit.

Ingredients:

- 1 tbsp extra virgin oil
- 5 medium egg yolks
- 375 mls of double cream
- 3 banana shallots finely chopped
- 7 oz of Strathdon blue cheese crumbled
- salt & pepper to taste
- 1 tbsp of chopped dill
- 2 tbsp of chopped parsley
- 1 tbsp of chopped chives
- 125 mls of milk

Method:

Preheat oven to 160 °C

Soften the shallots in the olive oil. (7-10 mins)

In a bowl, whisk eggs then the cream & milk

Combine the cheese, the softened shallots, herbs, and a few turns of salt & pepper to the mixture.

Pour into small ramekins & place in a bain marie for 30-40 mins or until just set in the middle.

'Brulée with a blow torch' with a 'super light' coating of icing sugar.

Makes about nine ramekins.

STRATHDON BLUE CHEESE BISCUITS

Ingredients:

50g butter   50g self raising flour   50g Strathdon blue cheese

Method:

- Pulse in a food processor the butter & flour then add the cheese and mix until fully combined and roll into a ball. Wrap in cling film & leave in fridge for around 30 minutes.
- Bring out of fridge & roll into small table tennis ball size.
- roll in oatmeal or sesame seeds
- bake in oven at 180 C for 15-20 mins until golden brown

PEAR & SAFFRON COMPOTE

Ingredients:

100ml cider   3 tbsp caster sugar

25g butter   ½ tspn saffron

3 large pears, Conference, Williams or Comice (approx. 600g)

Method:

- Boil cider & reduce by half (set aside to cool)
- Quarter, core & peel the pears into large chunks. Melt the butter and sugar and cook to a light caramel colour.
- Add pears & saffron & cook uncovered for 5 mins.
- Cover with wet greaseproof paper for 10 mins over reduced heat.
- Blend to a puree with the apple reduction (cider or spirit)

Gordon Davidson

BLACK AND GREEN OLIVES IN A GARLIC MARINADE

There is nothing better than sitting on the patio in the summer evenings relaxing with friends enjoying a large gin and tonic or/and a glass of wine and chatting and laughing and enjoying a selection of nibbles. If you actually like olives (after all, I am told they 'are an acquired taste!') then this is a quick and easy recipe.

Preparation Time – 10 minutes   Time to Serve - Minimum 1 hour

Utensils:

    Spoon   Mixing bowl

    Knife   Chopping board

    Glass   Small serving bowl

Ingredients:

    Gin   100g Pitted Black Olives

    Tonic   100g Pitted Green Olives

    Ice   2 Cloves Garlic - Sliced

    Lime   2 Tbsp Parsley - Chopped

    2 Tbsp Lemon Juice   2 Tbsp Basil - Chopped

    3-4 Tbsp of Olive Oil

½ tsp Chilli Pepper Flakes or ½ seeded and Finely Chopped Red Jalapeño

Method:

- First pour a large measure of gin into the glass
- Add tonic
- Add slice of lime and ice
- Sip
- Next gather all the remaining ingredients and chop and pour as above and put all together into the bowl and stir
- Cover and refrigerate for a minimum of 1 hour. Can be left to marinade for up to a day
- Sit in the evening sun until the guests arrive and finish gin and tonic
- When ready to serve transfer olives into the small bowl and serve
- As an alternative add small cubes of feta cheese or a chopped roasted pepper to the mixture.

If however, you do not have enough time to prepare the olives above or you can't be bothered with all that faffing, on your way home from work call at your local supermarket and purchase a selection of marinated olives from the deli counter. Transfer to the small serving bowls and no-one will be any the wiser!

Jo King

DECADENT SANDWICH.

Ingredients:

    2 slices of seeded wholemeal bread of your choice

    Brown sugar   1 Banana   Clotted cream

Method:

- Squash the banana onto one slice of bread and sprinkle with the brown sugar (as much or as little as you want).
- Spread the other slice of bread with clotted cream (as much or as little as you want).
- Put both slices together with the sticky mess on the inside.
- Cut into 2 (or 4 if that's your bag) and enjoy.

Willy Gofar

REG RAGGON RAREBIT

Can be grilled either on bread (with one side toasted already, obviously) or without, on a sturdy (grill-proof) plate:

The best cheese to use in my view is a mature cheddar, Red Leicester, Double Gloucester or a white crumbly cheese such as Caerphilly or Cheshire. Cut into thin-ish slices, covering the whole of the bread/ inner of the plate.

Then add the following, to taste:

    Worcester sauce   Tabasco (a little)   Ground black pepper

    English Mustard Powder (ready-made mustard can be used)

If desired, any one or more of the following options can be added:

A poached egg Baked beans   Sliced, grilled fresh tomatoes

Reg Raggon

CHEESE STRAWS A LA BOBBERS

Ingredients:

100g (4oz) Plain Flour	½ Tspn mustard powder
50g (2oz) Butter	½ Tspn paprika
1 egg yolk	Pinch of salt
Cold water to mix	50g (2oz) Strong cheddar cheese finely grated

Method:

- Preheat oven to 200°C / 400°F / Gas mark 6

- Sift together the flour, mustard powder, salt and paprika. Rub the butter into the flour until the mixture resembles breadcrumbs

- Mix in the cheese, then add the egg yolk and enough cold water to make a stiff but not sticky dough.

- Roll out the dough until it is about ½ centimetre (¼") thick. Trim the edges and cut into strips about 1 centimetre (½") wide.

- At this point, if you're planning to store your cheese straws in a container, it's a good idea to check the length of your container to make sure they will fit – now is the time to make them shorter if you need to.

- Place the cheese straws on a lightly greased baking tray and cook for 10-15 minutes until they look done. Light golden brown is what you're aiming for, if they're still pale and squishy looking they're not done yet, if they've gone black then they're probably a bit overdone.

- Remove the baking tray from the oven and leave to cool for a few minutes before transferring to a wire rack to cool completely. Please note that any cheese straws that get broken during this transfer are the perks of the cook, and contain less calories as some leak out when they break.

Best served with a bottle of red wine and some good friends

Bobcat (The Girlie)

SPAGHETTI CHEESE on TOAST

Wotcha Tel, how are you doing?

How's the recipe seeking going?

Thought I'd just put pen to pad,

And send one of mine for you to add.

It's one of my gran's from days of old,

But follow it through it's as good as gold

Take some bread & make into toast,

She used home made, but that's just a boast.

You can use shop bought if you want to be quick,

But always be sure and cut it thick.

Whilst it's browning take a pan,

And put in spaghetti straight from the can.

Put the toast out on a plate,

Spread with butter, don't hesitate.

Cover with pasta and lots of cheese,

Then brown under the grill and it's sure to please.

It's the perfect snack when watching Telly

And you're suffering from rumbling in the belly.

Don't give a thought to putting on weight,

Or the fact that you're eating far too late.

Just remember while you're enjoying your feed,

You're actually helping CHILDREN IN NEED.

Ida Bunny Noven

SCALLOP, AVOCADO and BACON SALAD

Ingredients: serves 2

8 scallops with coral	1 avocado
2 spring onions	juice of ½ lemon
4 slices lightly smoked streaky bacon	small leaf lettuce

for the dressing

1 tbsp white wine vinegar	1 tsp Dijon mustard
4 tbsp olive oil	1 dssp balsamic vinegar
1 tsp sugar vinegar	2 tbsp walnut oil

Method:

- Make up the dressing in a screw top jar and set aside
- Peel avocado and slice, squeeze lemon juice over slices to prevent discolouration
- Chop bacon and fry at high heat until crispy
- Remove from pan with a slotted spoon and drain on kitchen paper, leaving the bacon fat in the pan to fry the scallops in later
- Take a large bowl and put some dressing into it
- Put in salad leaves and mix by hand
- Put on 2 plates with avocado and chopped spring onions and drizzle some more dressing over the salad
- Fry the scallops at a very high heat for about 30 seconds each side and place on top of salad

Serve immediately

Sir Terry Wogan

SPANNER SALMON

Fear not this recipe does not include actual spanners (I know most of you realise that but you have to be so careful these days!) The reason this dish is so called is because it has orange and gin in the recipe. As orange and vodka is a screwdriver, I thought orange and gin would be a spanner... well it makes sense to me!

Anyway chefs hats on everyone it's time to make Spanner Salmon

Ingredients:

    One large piece of fresh salmon (about 750g)

    One nice juicy orange

    Lug of best gin

    Seasoning

    2 tsps olive oil

    Half a glass of water

Method:

- Preheat the oven on high for 20 minutes to warm up.

- Wash the salmon to remove any yucky bits and set aside. Make sure you use the freshest salmon you can get. If you are fusspot remove the bones with a pair of tweezers. Personally I can't be bothered

- Wash the outside of the orange to make sure it is clean if need be and then cut the orange in half and squeeze the juice out of it.

- Season the base of a wide shallow baking dish. Pour on half the orange juice.

- Now place the salmon in the dish skin side down (no pun intended – though if you want to intend a pun it is entirely up to you).

- Season again and pour over the lug of gin, the rest of the orange juice, and the olive oil.

- Pour in the water around the outside of the salmon. You don't want too much so use your own judgement. I like to put the juiced orange halves in the corners of the dish, but this is optional.

- Cover the dish with tin foil.

- Place the dish in the oven and bake for about 20 minutes. Then check the fish with a knife to see how well it is done. If it is very 'clear' in the middle it will need another 20 minutes or so. It all depends on how thick the fish is. You want the fish to be about 90% opaque because it will continue to cook in its own heat.

- When the fish is done you can either serve it hot from the oven with some nice hot new potatoes and peas, or allow it to cool and then bung it in the fridge to have the next day with a lovely potato salad.

Tigger

DESMOND'S FAVOURITE: CULLEN SKINK

A skink is a Scottish beef soup, but Cullen is a fishing village in Morayshire and so it is made from haddock instead. You can use smoked fish but I prefer a simple fresh haddock fillet.

Stuff:

- 1lb large haddock fillet(s)
- 1 large onion
- 1½lbs potatoes (a floury variety is best)
- 1 cup of milk (more or less)
- 1 tps ground dried bay leaves
- lumps of butter
- salt & pepper to taste
- Chopped parsley (for garish garnish)
- Single cream (about 2 tsp per person)

This is an unreconstructed politically incorrect recipe and therefore all measurements are in imperial sizes. None of the measures need be at all accurate and you should vary them according to your personal taste. Some versions of the recipe insist on double the amount of haddock, so it is up to you.

Doings:

Coarsely chop the onion, think of your first love affair and weep copious tears.

Clean (and peel if you wish) the potatoes and put in boiling salted water until soft enough to mash.

Whilst the potatoes cook, place the fish in a shallow pan of boiling water (just enough to cover the fish) and simmer for about five minutes.

The fish will begin to break up. Take the pan off the boil and use a spatula to break it up into flakes in the water. Add the onion and ground bay leaves, salt and pepper to taste.

Put the pan back on the heat and simmer for 15 minutes, stirring from time to time.

Mash the potatoes. When the onions have truly softened, pour in the milk and begin to add tablespoons of the mashed potato, stirring all the time. Continue to add mash until the soup is the thickness you require, (I like it quite thick and creamy). Add more milk if you need extra fluid. Check the seasoning, you will find the bay leaves have made it quite hot and spicy – this is good.

Continue to simmer and stir occasionally until you are ready or for about ½ an hour. Serve in pretentious rustic bowls, add a teaspoonful or so of single cream and stir one turn to make a spiral in the soup, add a knob of butter to each bowl and sprinkle with chopped parsley.

Serve with tasteful tiny triangles of toast if you live in north London and this is a dinner party; otherwise serve with huge chunks of fresh bread and butter (other spreads are available).

The soup will freeze for later and it is a brilliant winter warmer equal to at least one extra cardigan.

Desmond Carrington
Perthshire - July 2008

ANDREW'S FISH PIE

Ingredients:

    35gr. Onions, finely chopped   30gr. Spinach

    35gr. Carrots, finely chopped   100ml. Double cream

    25gr. Mature Cheddar   50gr. Mashed potatoes

    1 tspn Extra Virgin Olive Oil   Small splash Dry Sherry

200gr. Cod, Salmon & Smoked Haddock - cut in Strips "Fish Finger" size

Good pinch of Flat-leaf Parsley, chopped and sprinkled.

Method:

- Sweat Onions & Carrot with olive oil in a saucepan with a tight fitting lid.
- Remove from heat and shock with cold sherry.
- Transfer to a pie dish.
- Lay alternate fingers of fish on top.
- Cover with either frozen or blanched fresh spinach, top with chopped parsley, cheese and cream.
- Pipe mashed potatoes around the edge and a rosette in the middle.
- Bake in the oven at 180c. for 30 mins.

Andrew Hatton

KNIGHTSBRIDGE PIE

My Mum used to make this about 40 years ago. I found the recipe the other day hidden in an old cookbook.

Her Ladyship has volunteered to make it and remind me of my teenage years. I've forgotten what it tastes like now (but then I forget most things these days!)

Cook & Enjoy....

Ingredients:

- ¾ lb of boiled potatoes
- ½ lb of cooked white fish
- Tin of flaked tuna
- Large tin of peas.
- Packet of white sauce mix, made up.

Method:

- Grease a large pie dish and slice 1/3 of the pre-cooked potatoes into a layer on the bottom.
- Put a layer using all the cooked flaked white fish on top of this along with ½ the tinned peas, followed by some more of the potatoes.
- Put a layer of tuna on top of this along with the rest of the peas. Top this with the potatoes.
- Pour over the white sauce put some knobs of butter on the top and place in an oven for 25 mins at Gas mark 4. (170 C)
- Garnish with chopped parsley and serve.

LORD ELPUSS of YARNFIELD STAFFS

(Plus some assistance from the good Lady Jane)

CHEESE BAKED FISH

Ingredients:

200g fish fillets (I use cod or haddock but any white fish is alright)

Small onion

Large tin chopped tomatoes

1 tbsp cooking oil

Salt and pepper

1 tsp mixed herbs

40g breadcrumbs brown or white

80g cheese - strong one such as Red Leicester works best

Method:

- Place fish in bottom of ovenproof dish. Sprinkle with salt and pepper.
- Peel and chop onion finely. Heat oil in pan and fry onion gently for few minutes, without browning.
- Add tomatoes and herbs to pan. Simmer for 10 minutes.
- Make breadcrumbs using blender. Grate cheese. Mix breadcrumbs and cheese together.
- Pour tomato mixture over fish.
- Cover evenly with breadcrumbs and cheese.
- Bake at Gas 4 or 180C for 30 minutes or until top is golden brown.

Edina Cloud

PRAWNS PIL-PIL

Serves 4, in individual gratin dishes.

Ingredients:

    Uncooked prawns, 6-8 large per person (cut in half)

    300ml Extra Virgin Olive Oil   Pinch of Paprika

    Glug of Chilli Oil (optional)   Salt & Pepper

    4 Large Cloves of Garlic sliced, plus 2 more crushed

    2 whole fresh Red Chillies, seeds removed, finely chopped

    Handful of chopped flat-leaf Parsley

Serve with bread: a large French stick, sliced then halved

Method:

- Put both oils, all of the garlic. chilli, paprika, salt & pepper into a large frying pan or wok. If possible, do this earlier in the day… boil for a minute whilst stirring, then switch off the heat to allow to infuse for a few hours
- Put your serving dishes into a hot oven half an hour before serving to get them as hot as you can.
- When you're ready to cook… Dry prawns with kitchen roll, & bring oil up to a boil, but don't allow it to smoke.
- Drop in the prawns, get the oil bubbling again. Stirring occasionally, cook for about 5 mins.
- They will be ready about a minute or so after all the prawns have turned pink all over. Turn off the heat & throw in the parsley.
- Place your hot serving dishes on top of a napkin on a flat plate, to serve.
- With a slotted serving spoon carefully divide the prawns between the bowls, then pour on all of the hot oil/chilli/garlic mixture over the prawns.

Seymour Paunch

EEL EN CROUTE

This is a dish traditionally prepared by young men from London's east end for that extra special girl on that important first date.

(However, be warned that in my experience not all young women are prepared for the delicate flavours involved and sometimes rush for the front door with their hands clasped over their mouths when the dish is presented. It may be that they were not prepared for the subtle aroma of the croute.)

First you will need a very fresh large eel, preferably from the river Lea or the middle reaches of the Thames. Avoid those from Barking Creek as they can at time import strange flavours. If you take the trouble to shop for your eel at Walthamstow High Street Market, you will be able to obtain a live eel from the stall there. You will then be able to keep it in the bath until you are ready to dispatch it. (Check the bath if necessary to avoid the possibility of tainting the eel with shower gel)

Stun or dispatch your eel by whichever method you prefer. Personally I find plugging it into a 13-amp circuit works well and produces an electric eel effect.

Then nail your eel to the back door, just below the head in preparation for the careful skinning process. (You may prefer to use somebody else's back door as, to be honest, the process can be a trifle messy)

Using a small, very sharp knife carefully slit the skin of the eel around the circumference about 6" from the head and repeat the process about 6" from the tip of the tail. Slit along the stomach of the eel to join both slits. At this point, you can then degut your eel and let the innards drop into a bucket. (You may wish to keep the bucket handy in case your chosen dinner companion is one of those who does not enjoy the smell of the croute.)

Parboil your eel for a few minutes but keep the liquid, as this will form the basis of the famous glutinous green salty flavour beloved by easterners as the gravy enjoyed with eels.

Carefully unwrap your purchased puff pastry and roll out to the length of the portion of the eel between the slits.

Using household pliers grip the slit edge and pulling firmly downwards skin your eel. You should then be left with the 6" of eel head complete with skin then a length of naked skinned eel ending in a tail complete with skin.

Roll the puff pastry around the skinned section of the eel, sealing and coating with beaten egg. You should finish up with what looks like a long raw sausage roll with an eel head and tail sticking out of each end.

Place on an oiled 36" baking tray and place in a preheated very wide oven Gas Mark 7 / 220 C for 20 minutes then lower to GM 4 / 180 C so the filling is cooked.

Remove and serve immediately after chopping into 1-foot lengths with a sharp cleaver and removing the spine and spinal cord.

Serve with green liquor poured liberally over mashed potatoes and boiled asparagus.

Accompany with a crisp dry cold Chablis Premier Cru.

Warning... If intending to catch your own eel or wishing to obtain one from a freelance supplier, please ensure it is not one of the large reef living varieties.

Keeping a conger or moray eel in the bath and subsequently trying to nail on to your back door is possibly not recommended.

Ricky T Outhouse.

KEL'S CHICKEN & BROCCOLI BAKE

Ingredients

- 3 skinned chicken breast fillets - cubed / sliced
- 1 head of broccoli
- 200g button mushrooms
- 280ml double cream (can use elmlea or other reduced fat double cream)
- 1 tin of Campbells condensed chicken or mushroom soup (again I use the fat-free one)
- 1 tsp mild curry powder (if you like things spicier either add more, or use hotter curry)
- Bread crumbs (these can be homemade, those bright orange ones, or wholemeal!)

Method

- Preheat the oven to 200°C gas mark 6
- Quick fry your chicken to seal it - it doesn't have to be fully cooked, but should be white all over the outside.
- Break up the broccoli into smaller florets - not too small else they'll disintegrate, but the right size for the eater to pop in their mouth without cutting.
- Lightly sauté the mushrooms in a little butter - so just coloured.
- Turn the chicken, broccoli and mushrooms into an ovenproof dish - I use a rectangular earthenware lasagne style dish.
- Empty the cream into a jug. Whisk in the soup and curry powder.

- Pour resultant mix over the chicken, broccoli and mushrooms, ensuring everything is covered.
- Sprinkle breadcrumbs over the whole thing - and bake in the middle of the oven for 25 - 30 minutes.

Serve with a mixed salad and rice or cous-cous (it goes well with lemon & coriander).

Serves 4

Kelly Sigh

LEMON CHICKEN with HAM

Take a chicken breast for each person

Season with pepper and wrap in piece of cured ham (Cumbrian Black Ham works really well, but any other good quality ham would work)

Put in a baking dish with slices of lemon over the top to keep the chicken succulent

Put more slices of ham over the top just to stop burning

Mix lemon juice and olive oil with a teaspoon of dried mustard and pour around the chicken

Cook in the oven for about 40 minutes at 200 C / gas mark 6

Serve with steamed vegetables (asparagus, beans and carrot work well) and a few baby new potatoes

Glen B Ogle

DERRY'S CHICKEN CURRY

Ingredients:

- 6 Chicken thighs
- 2 onions (chopped)
- 4 cloves garlic (crushed)
- 2 tspn turmeric
- 1 lump root ginger (fine chopped)
- 1½ tspn chilli
- 6 cardamom pods
- 1 large tub natural yoghurt
- 1 mixed handful coriander & mint
- oil
- 50gms / large chunk coconut block (chopped)

Method:

- Heat oil. Fry onions and garlic. Add turmeric, mix. Add chicken + ¼ cup of water, cook for 5 mins.
- Add ginger, chilli and cardamom pods, cook for 5 mins, take off heat.
- Mix the coconut with ½ the yoghurt in a bowl and add to the pan, mix gently.
- Cover and cook on a very low heat for 1 hr stirring occasionally. Take lid off and continue cooking to reduce liquid.
- When sauce is gloopy, mix the coriander & mint with the rest of the yoghurt and add to the pan, stir in and serve

Lorien Van Parc

HONEY AND GARLIC CHICKEN

Our dear friends Allan and Eleanor lived in a rose-covered cottage in 10 acres of Sussex countryside. They were so keen for me to marry Chris that every time we walked round their little lake in the evening, they'd turn on the fairy lights in the hope that the romantic setting would make me say yes.
It clearly worked!

When the poppy flowers outside their breakfast room window had died and the seed heads were left, we'd come down in the morning to find Allan had drawn faces on them. It looked like a group of monks were peering in the window!

Eleanor would grill chicken joints that had been marinated for a few hours in the following ingredients:

    2/3 mug of clear honey

    1/3 mug of balsamic vinegar

    2 cloves of garlic crushed

    1 tsp mustard powder

    1 tsp marjoram

The marinade is used to baste the joints as they cook. You can also dot them with butter at the start of cooking.
They're delicious served with new potatoes and a fresh green salad.

Rev Ruth Scott
Top Ecclesiastical Totty

CHICKEN PASTA GARLIC SURPISE

A good one for using up leftovers, as long as none of them is even one second past the sell-by date, of course!

Ingredients:

Chicken breasts and/or thighs	Garlic
Red or Green pepper	Cherry tomatoes
Mixed Herbs	Butter
Dried Chilli Flakes or a fresh red chilli	Whatever pasta you fancy
Bottle of Gin	Bottle of Tonic

Method:

- Bake the chicken bits for about an hour, in foil, with a splash of olive oil and 2 or 3 cloves of garlic, at about 160c

- Mix the Gin and the Tonic in a glass and drink at leisure

- When the chicken is done, take it out and chop it up

- Cook the pasta as required

- While it is boiling, chop up a good handful of cherry tomatoes and some of the finely chopped red or green pepper and fry gently in some melted butter, along with a couple of cloves of finely chopped garlic. (Keep the heat moderate so the garlic doesn't burn)

- Give this mixture a couple of minutes' head start and then chuck in the chilli and a sprinkling of Mick Sturbs.

- Imbibe further G&T if required

- When the pasta is done, drain it and then add the chopped chicken and pour in the tomato/pepper/garlic/chilli/butter mixture from the frying pan.

- Stir well and add freshly ground black pepper to taste. Drizzle with some olive oil.

Tip: Make a big load of this, resolving to keep some aside for the next day. Then scoff the lot.

Charles "Bossa Nova" Nove

TUNA PIE

Method:

- Put Tuna in oven proof dish and cover with cheese sauce
- Cover with mashed potatoes and then a layer of grated cheese
- Bake in oven until golden brown
- Can add some crumbled crisps on top after.

Love Lollie XXXX

TAMARIND CHICKEN NOODLES

Ingredients:

- 1 pack fine egg noodles
- 2 chicken breasts, boned thighs or some leftover chicken, shredded
- 1 pack Pak Choi, sliced and washed (can be gritty)
- Couple of spring onions, sliced

For marinade:

2 cloves garlic, grated	Juice of ½ lime
1 tbsp soy sauce	1 tbsp fish sauce (Nam Pla)
1 tbsp brown sugar or honey	2 tbsp oil
1 tsp tamarind paste	1 red chilli, deseeded and finely chopped, or 1 tsp chilli flakes

Method:

- Slice a couple of chicken breasts into strips, mix all the marinade ingredients together in a bowl and add the chicken, turning it over so it's all combined. Leave to one side while you boil a saucepan of water, salt it and pop in your noodles.

- Heat a wok or large saucepan and throw in the chicken together with all the marinade (it's got oil in so you shouldn't need any more) and the spring onions. Stir-fry until the chicken's cooked, it doesn't take long. Add your chopped Pak Choi near the end – this really needs just to be warmed through, it's horrible if it's soggy - and toss together.

- Drain your noodles and tip them into the wok, mixing them all in with the chicken and the sauce. Serve sprinkled with chopped salted peanuts and some coriander.

By the way, if you want to make this more like chicken noodle soup, boil the noodles in 1 litre of made-up chicken stock, cook the chicken separately, then add it all in to the noodles at the end.

Rita Fantham

HERBY LAMB KANERBY

Take a sharp knife and stab your lamb joint several times.

If you have some fresh garlic, slices can be inserted into some of the slits.

Cover the leg with runny honey.

Add the following, to taste:

Oregano   Rosemary   Dried mint   Cracked black pepper

Herbs de Provence and/or mixed herbs   Sea salt

Mustard powder (or ready-made mustard, either English or Dijon)

Half a glass of red wine (to cook the leg in; the other half of the glass can be drunk, if desired)

Can also be garnished with bay leaves

Suggested accompaniments:
(can be cooked around the roasting leg):

Aubergine (medium to thick cut)

Tomatoes (cherry or preferably plum cherries - on the vine if available)

Mushrooms (shiitakes, if you can pronounce them)

Parsnips (thin and crispy - cheat and use frozen ones if out of season)

A mixture of potatoes and sweet potatoes, diced small to medium

Cook in a medium to hot oven for a little longer than the weight of the leg would suggest.

Reg Raggon

CURRIED LAMB SHANKS

Serves 4

Like any curry, this is best made the day before. Marinade the lamb the day before cooking. Re-heat at gas mark 4 for one hour.

Serve with Anya potatoes or baby new potatoes, tossed in butter.

Ingredients:

- 4 lamb shanks
- 5 large cloves garlic, crushed
- 2 tbsp hot madras curry paste
- 150ml chicken stock
- 2 large mild onions
- ½ cup sultanas
- ½ fresh lemon, sliced
- groundnut oil, salt & pepper
- 2 large (or 3 medium) cooking apples, peeled & chopped
- 6 plum tomatoes, skinned & de-seeded, cut into 1 inch pieces

Marinade:

- 1 tbsp each of dried ground coriander, cumin, & medium curry powder
- 1 tsp each of dried rosemary & thyme
- ½ tsp each of salt & pepper

Method for marinade:

- grind all of the above finely & add 2 tbsp olive oil
- coat the lamb, put into a strip-seal bag, & refrigerate overnight

Method:

- Pre-heat oven to Gas Mk 4 / 180 C
- Wipe off as much marinade as possible from the lamb.
- Brown the meat in a little groundnut oil, in a large over-proof pan. Remove the lamb to a warm dish.
- Add a little more oil to the pan if dry, stir in curry paste & cook gently for 2 minutes.
- Add onions, cook for 5 minutes. Add garlic, cook for 2 more minutes.
- Put meat back into the pan. Add lemon, apple, sultanas, stock, salt & pepper.
- Turn up the heat for a minute on the hob, put lid on & into the oven for 2 ½ hours.
- Remove from oven & stir in tomatoes.
- Serve it up or preferably cool & refrigerate till next day, then re-heat.

Seymour Paunch

ROASTED RUMP OF LAMB, BUBBLE & SQUEAK with TOMATO & ROSEMARY CHUTNEY.

Ingredients:

- 1 Lamb Rump 8oz
- 10 Fresh Tomatoes
- 2 Red Onions
- 1 Savoy Cabbage
- 4 Sprigs of Rosemary
- 4 Potatoes
- 1 White Onion
- 4 Slices of Bacon
- 8oz Brown Sugar
- 4oz Butter

Method:

- Peel the potatoes put in water and boil until soft, then drain.
- Slice the white onion, cut up the bacon, slice half of the savoy cabbage, put all these in a pan and gently 'sweat off'.
- Seal off the lamb in a pan with hot oil, then place in the oven at 180C and cook for 10 minutes.
- Dice the 10 tomatoes with the 2 red onions and put in a pan with 8oz of brown sugar and cook until soft and 'chutney like' then add 4 sprigs of rosemary.
- When the lamb is cooked leave to 'rest' for approximately 5 minutes.
- Mash the potatoes and add 4oz butter and the cooked bacon, onion and cabbage and season to taste.
- Place the bubble and squeak mixture in the centre of plate.
- Slice the lamb into 4 slices and place on the bubble and squeak, then dress the plate with the tomato & rosemary chutney.

Stephen Monks
Head Chef - The Bellingham

EASY & POSH ONE POT CASSEROLE

Ingredients:

    Braising steak in small pieces

    Onions, finely chopped

    Mushrooms, sliced

    Pepper, diced (whatever colour you fancy)

    Carton of orange juice.

Method:

- Put all the ingredients into a large casserole dish, cover with orange juice, seal with foil and put into the oven. About gas mark 5 or about 175 C, or whatever temperature you usually cook with.
- Leave for a couple of hours then serve with green beans and baked potatoes, or new potatoes or whatever you feel like!

Ps: always ask your guest to guess the mystery ingredient; they don't usually work it out!

Rhea Juvenate

BEEF AND PARSNIP PIE

Ingredients:

BASE

    5 Medium (about 750g) Parsnips chopped

    20g Butter   2 tablespoons of milk

FILLING

    1 Tbsp oil   1 Onion, chopped

    2 Carrots, chopped (diced)   1 can Chopped Tomatoes

    500g Minced Beef (any kind of mince will do just as well)

    1 Oxo cube   2 Tbsp tomato paste

    Salt and Pepper

TOPPING

    2 Slices dried toast (To make into breadcrumbs)

    2oz Tasty cheese (Grated)

Method:

BASE

- Boil parsnips until tender
- Drain and mash with the milk and butter until smooth.
- Spread the mixture over the base and sides of a **greased** pie dish, (approx. 9in)

FILLING

- Heat oil in a pan and cook the onions until soft.
- Add the carrot and mince together and cook, stirring, until the mince is browned.
- Add the can of chopped tomatoes, crumbled stock cube, and paste.
- Add salt and pepper to taste.
- Bring to the boil and then simmer uncovered for about 15 minutes until most of the liquid has evaporated.
- Spread the filling over the parsnip base.

TOPPING

- Combine the breadcrumbs and cheese in a bowl.
- Sprinkle over the filling.
- Bake uncovered, in a moderate oven for about 20-30 minutes or until brown.

NOTE: If there is to be quite a wait between making the pie and putting it in the oven to bake then sprinkle the filling with about 3/4 of the grated cheese while it is still hot. Mix the remainder of the cheese with the breadcrumbs and sprinkle this over the top of the pie before putting it in to bake. This will give a nice crispy covering to the pie.

Jack Nifedlorry

BEEF IN HORSERADISH SAUCE

Ingredients:

    2lb chuck/stewing steak   2 small onions, sliced

    Knob of butter & splash of oil   2 tspn garam masala

    1 tspn ground ginger   1 pint beef stock

    1tbspn creamed horseradish   ½tspn sugar

    5ozs soured cream or yoghurt   ½tspn salt

Method:

- Heat oven to gas mark 3 (170C)
- On the hob, brown steak in the butter and oil for 5 minutes. Stir in the garam masala, ginger, sugar and salt.
- Add the sliced onion, Worcestershire sauce and beef stock. Bring to the boil and simmer for 5 mins.
- Transfer to a lidded casserole and cook in the oven for 2 ½ - 3hrs.
- When cooked, remove from oven and stir in horseradish sauce and soured cream or yoghurt.
- Leave to stand for 10mins before serving.
- If necessary, gently re-heat on the hob taking care that the cream does not curdle.

Serve with veg with lots of red wine to drink.

Lorien Van Parc

RUMP IN DOG (OR BBQ STEAK IN ALE)

Dog here refers to Newcastle Brown Ale (also known as Newcie Broon or Jawney Inta Space)! This recipe is quite good for a BBQ party as the steak stretches further than normal.

Make a marinade of Broon Ale (you can use other dark beers), a good slug of soy sauce and a dash of Worcester Sauce. Add a couple of teaspoons of sugar and three crushed and chopped cloves of garlic. Season with salt and pepper.

Take some reasonably thick rump steak and cut it into 1/2" wide strips.

Beat these with a meat mallet or rolling pin until fairly thin (they will recover a bit) and add to the marinade.

Put in the fridge for up to 24 hours before barbecuing.

Glen B Ogle

TURKISH GREEN BEAN STEW

Ingredients: For 2 Servings:

2 tbsp Olive Oil	6-8 tomatoes - grated
1 green chilli – deseeded	1 clove garlic - finely chopped
½ onion, finely chopped	½ tspn honey
1 teaspoon Italian Herbs	Juice of 1 lemon
1lb Green Beans - prepared and cut into 1" bits	
Salt & Pepper to taste	

Method:

- Sauté the onions gently in the oil for 4-5 mins. Add chilli, garlic and herbs, stir and cook for 1 minute. Add tomatoes and lemon juice, bring to the boil and then add the beans.
- Cover and simmer for up to half an hour. Add honey and season to taste. Serve.

Lorien Van Parc

EASY MINUTE STEAK

Very simple and easy to make, with a twist!

Ingredients:

- 2-4 minute steaks (beef)
- seasoning
- cider or balsamic vinegar

Method:

- Take your grill pan and sprinkle on seasoning: sea salt & black pepper, chilli if you wish!
- Place the minute steaks (or use thinly cut steaks) on the grill pan, and this time seasoning the meat. This method enables you to season both sides without any fuss.
- Pour 2 tsps of the vinegar of your choice over each steak, (on one side only).
- Grill the meat, turning once for about 4 minutes each side (this will depend on the thickness of the steaks - I am not one for bloodied meat, so I like my steak well done).
- Serve immediately with a crisp green salad.

Tigger

Corned Beef En Croute

Ingredients:

- One packet of puff pastry
- One tin of corned beef

Method:

- Roll out pastry,
- Open tin of corned beef (Very important!)
- Wrap corned beef in pastry
- Bung in oven for 25 minutes.

I actually saw this done by TV weatherman Fred Talbot many years ago.

An old Romany Recipe from Gypsy Petrolengine

Editor's note – you might have to experiment a few times on oven temperatures!

BRAISED BRISKET of BEEF
Slow Cooker Style

Ingredients:

    2 - 3lb rolled brisket   Good pinch mixed herbs

    1 large onion chopped   Salt & Pepper

    2 stick celery chopped   Bay leaf

    3 medium carrots sliced   1 dsp plain flour

    Oil for frying/browning meat

    1 (or 2) bottle red wine (Merlot, Corbierre or similar)

Method:

- Turn on Slow cooker to low setting.
- In large pan heat tablespoon oil.
- Pour large glass of wine.
- Start to brown joint.
  Slowly drink glass of wine until all surfaces of meat browned, place meat in slow cooker.
  If necessary place more oil in pan and heat.
- Pour another glass of wine.
  Add all vegetables to pan and brown slowly until wine is finished.
- Add dessertspoon of plain flour and stir into veg and oil.
  Pour another glass of wine and add to vegetables, stir until thickened. Should be consistency of single cream; add more wine or water to thin if necessary.
- Season with mixed herbs, bay leaf and salt and pepper to taste.
  Add to meat in slow cooker.
  Pour another glass of wine, put lid on cooker and leave for up to 6 hours.

- Sit down and relax and finish glass of wine, if any left finish bottle.

- Set timer for about 5 hours, go to sleep.
  On waking check meat for tenderness, should be OK after this time, if not repeat wine and cooking process for another hour or so.

- Open another bottle of wine and pour large glass.
  If sauce too thin thicken with cornflour. If too thick thin sauce with a little water.
  Slowly drink wine and check seasoning of sauce.

- Remove meat and serve sliced with sauce separate, goes well with red wine and boiled new potatoes and green beans.
  Also tastes good cold as you may fall asleep again after carving.

Elsan Buckett
Chef extraordinaire

Sweet Stuff
I love you my treacle tart,
You are the apple of my pie,
You can make my rhubarb crumble,
Your cherry dumplings please the eye,
You are the crème of my brulee,
You're no gooseberry fool my lover,
So how about an Ice Cream on Sunday,
And some roly poly under the cover!

Tudor Raincoat

TACO 'SOUP'

Ingredients:

1 tin of chopped tomatoes	1 small tin of sweetcorn
1 tin of red kidney beans	8 oz of minced beef
1 small onion, chopped	1 clove of garlic, crushed
2 tbsp of tomato puree	1 packet of taco seasoning
Plain yoghurt or sour cream	2 tbsp cooking oil

Method:

- Gently fry the garlic and onions together for 5 minutes then add the beef. Continue cooking for 10 minutes
- Open the tins, drain the beans and sweetcorn, and put contents of all 3 into a saucepan large enough to hold them, along with the puree and seasoning.
- Stir and heat the mixture and then add the cooked beef and onion.
- Cover and cook gently for 30 minutes,.
- Serve hot with a spoonful of yoghurt or sour cream, accompanied with garlic bread or rice.
- I suggest you try this yourself (if you like spicy food) as I was not impressed when presented with it in New York last year, until I tasted it!

P E Dant

HAMBURGERS WITH SMOKEY BACON AND SUNDRIED TOMATOES
(Makes 16)

Ingredients:

    2lbs lean ground steak

    3 x rashers smoked bacon
    fat removed and chopped fairly finely

    5 or 6 Sundried tomatoes in oil,
    drained and fairly finely chopped

    Several good shakes breadcrumbs

    2 eggs

    Good grind black pepper

    Good blob brown sauce

    Good sprinkle bbq seasoning

    ½ tsp. salt

    2 x medium onions, finely chopped

Method:
- Mix all the ingredients together
- Make into 16 rounds and flatten into burgers
- Chill
- Grill or bbq

Carol Dickens

MR MINCE'S CONVENTION SURVIVAL MINCE
as dictated to Lucy Quipment

(Or what the ex Rusty E Quipment lives on when Lucy Quipment's away - no prizes for guessing why he's now known as Mr Mince)

Ingredients:

    2lb lean mince. Or, when confused, 2 kilos of lean mince.

    1 bag large potatoes, - cut in large chunks

    2-3 large onions - cut in chunks

    1 neep - the big thing with the orange flesh - cut in chunks

    A handful of carrots - about 6 - cut in chunks

    2 mealie puddings / mealie jimmies / white pudding / oatmeal pudding / Hog's pudding (other dialect names are available) as optional extras

It's hard to be definite about the quantity of vegetables, as much depends on how big your pan(s) is/are and how much room you've got left.

Method:

- Brown mince in its own juice in the biggest pan you've got. If you've made a mistake and got 2 kilos instead of 2lb, because you're a Tog and pre-decimal, spread among several pans.

- Slice onions ½ inch thick and lay on top of mince. Let them cook for a bit then stir them in.

- Make stock using Bisto granules, and a wee bit of black pepper. Add salt if you want. Don't make the stock too thin.

- Add the stock to the mince, and bring to the boil.

- Add the other vegetables, filling the pan but leaving stirring room.

- If you have the room and the inclination, lay a couple of mealie jimmies on top. Wrap one in foil to keep it whole, and leave the other au naturel so that it adds a je ne sais quoi to the gravy.

- Simmer on low heat for approx. 30 minutes, until tatties are cooked. Go and have a tune on the accordion while waiting.

Serving suggestion - Serve with a glass of good red wine, and a slab of bread to mop up the gravy.

As this recipe gets better with age like a good man (Mr Mince's words) dish the remainder of the mince into plastic storage boxes and put in fridge.

Take a serving from the fridge each subsequent day and reheat. Continue until the mince is gone, or you get fed up with mince in which case put it in the freezer.

Any pan scrapings should be placed in the dogs' dishes where they will be gratefully received.

Mr Mince
aka Rusty E Quipment

BOOBOOLONE
(three cheese pasta dish)

Ingredients:

- 4ozs dry pasta
- 1tbsp olive oil
- ½ onion, sliced
- 2 cloves garlic, chopped
- 1tsp fresh rosemary, chopped
- 2ozs ground beef
- 2ozs pork sausage meat

- 500g pasta sauce
- 3tbsp sour cream
- 6ozs mozzarella, shredded
- 4ozs Brie
- 2ozs Gorgonzola
- 2tsp fresh grated Parmesan

Method:

- Pre heat oven to 175C.
- Grease a 9 X 13inch baking dish or equivalent.
- Bring a large pan of lightly salted water to the boil. Add the pasta and cook for 8 - 10 mins or until al dente, then drain.
- Heat the oil in casserole dish and sauté the onion. Stir in the rosemary and garlic, then add the minced beef and sausage meat, cook until evenly browned.
- Add the pasta sauce and reduce to a slow simmer.
- In the prepared dish place half the pasta then layer the Brie, Gorgonzola, the sour cream and a little less than half of the meat mixture.
- Layer the rest of the pasta, mozzarella, the remaining meat mix and the Parmesan.
- Place in the preheated oven for 20 -30mins

Cara Van Parc

MUM'S SAUSAGE AND LENTIL CASSEROLE

Ingredients:

1lb (500g) Pork Sausages (cut into 1 inch/ 2.5cm chunks)

4 carrots (peeled and chop into wee chunks)

4 parsnips (peeled and chop into wee chunks)

4 med size tatties, peeled and chopped into wee chunks

1 or 2 red chillies (seeds removed and finely chop) these are optional

2 to 3 tbsp oil	3 onions (skin and chop)
1 lge garlic clove	8 ozs (250gms) lentils
2 pints (1.2 litres) chick or veg stock	Salt and pepper

Method:

- Grill sausages until brown all over.
- Heat oil in saucepan or large casserole and add onions.
- Fry gently for 4 to 5 mins then stir in carrots, parsnips, garlic, chillies and potatoes.
- Cook for a few minutes then stir in the lentils and browned sausages, stock and season.
- Cover saucepan or casserole dish with tight fitting lid and cook over low heat for 45 minutes until veggies are tender.

Best eaten on a cold day with loads of crusty bread and a nice bottle of wine!

Payne n' Diaz

CODDLE

Ingredients:

½ lb thin sausages	1 large onion
2 rashers bacon	1 large potato
tomato puree (lots)	½ stock cube
piri piri chicken seasoning	½ pint whole milk
½ pack knorr chilli con carne	mix clove garlic

frozen chopped chillies (I use 'very lazy chopped chilli' in jar)

(double up for 2 people)

Method:

- Chop onion and put in saucepan with milk; gently bring to boil with garlic & stock cube (milk will look curdled – don't worry).

- Cut up sausages into inch long pieces and add to milk and onion.

- Trim fat from bacon, cut into pieces and add to pan.

- Stir for a few seconds, add tomato puree and stir in, and then add rest of seasoning.
  Stir gently and add more milk if necessary.

- Cover and simmer gently for about 30 minutes.

- Peel potato and cut into small pieces. Boil until tender, drain and add to coddle mix.

(Dave's mum says the best of Irish luck – it looks like a dogs dinner!!)

Betty Dribbles
(I know the thought of sausages cooked in milk doesn't sound too appetising, but believe me, its yummy!!)

CHILLI PORK
A quick and tasty dish

Ingredients:

- 400-500g diced pork
- 100g diced chorizo
- 1 large thinly sliced onion
- 1 sliced red pepper
- 1 sliced yellow pepper
- 400g can chopped tomatoes
- 2 tsp paprika
- 1 tsp crushed chilli (from a jar)
- 10 - 15 halved green olives

Method:

- Cook the chorizo and onion together in a large pan until the onion is soft.
- Add the pork and peppers and cook for 5 minutes.
- Add the tomatoes, chilli and paprika. Cover and simmer for 20 minutes.
- Add the olives. Cover and simmer for another 10 minutes.
- Serve with rice.

Serves 4.

Penelaine

SPAMBALAYA

Ingredients:

Serves two (or nine in a home!)

1 tin of Spam (diced)	2 chopped red onions
2 chicken breasts (diced)	150g long grain rice
150g cooked & peeled prawns	Chopped cloves of garlic
2 sticks chopped celery	1 pint of chicken stock
Cayenne pepper	Oil
2 chopped bell peppers (any colour)	

As your taste buds may be at the stage where an oral zimmer frame is required, the quantities of cayenne pepper and garlic are left to your judgement

Method:

- Over a medium heat fry the chicken in a little oil until it colours.
- Add the celery, peppers, onion, garlic and the Spam, continue to fry for two minutes.
- Stir in the rice and and cayenne pepper.
- Add the stock (plus extra water, if required, to just cover ingredients)
- Increase heat and boil for 2 minutes, then simmer for ten minutes, then cover frying pan and turn off heat.
- Allow about ten minutes for most of liquid to be absorbed (if too much liquid remains quickly boil to reduce) then stir in prawns, re-cover for 1 minute and then serve

"Spamtastic!"

Phil Officer

Gina's Pheasant

Ingredients:

- 1 - 1½ pheasant breast per person, cut into strips
- 1-2 onions, chopped
- 2-3 tbs Worcestershire sauce
- 2-3 tbs mango chutney
- 1 small carton (¼ pint) double cream

Methods:

- Sweat onions until translucent in wok or large frying pan
- Remove and reserve onions, and brown pheasant strips
- Combine onions and pheasant, mix other ingredients together and continue cooking until meat is cooked through.
- Alternatively, oven cook browned pheasant breasts on bed of translucent onions, with sauce poured over, uncovered, for approx 20 minutes at 180°

Lucy Quipment

ITALIAN ALPINE PASTA SAUCE

Ingredients: - serves two

> 100grams or so of mushrooms, button or field are fine, not too exotic!
>
> About four rashers of dry cure smoked streaky bacon
>
> One small onion
>
> Two cloves of garlic (or to taste!)
>
> Five slices of pancetta (I tend to use a whole packet mind)
>
> Double cream (a good splash - or around half a small pot)
>
> Tomato passatta, about 250mls - enough to make the sauce
>
> Black Pepper - no salt as the bacon and pancetta is very salty
>
> 250 grams of your favourite pasta - dried is best for this (this is for two greedy people)

Method: - preparation

Ok - this recipe involves a lot of chopping, if you can get the ingredients to be very finely chopped, the recipe seems to work better, so....

- Finely chop the onion, mushrooms and garlic, to a point when the mushrooms look a little like "granules", keep the ingredients separate at this point
- Roll the bacon and chop finely
- Roll up the pancetta and also chop finely

Method: - cooking

- Put the pasta on to cook - a little al dente is good

- Heat up a frying pan with good sides or a non stick saucepan and add some vegetable oil

- Add the bacon and allow to cook until just a little coloured, then add the onion. Continue cooking until the onion has cooked through and only has a little colour.

- Add the mushrooms and carry on cooking until the mushrooms have released their moisture i.e. are cooked a bit and then add the garlic and the pancetta.

- Continue to cook until you have a dryish (but not dry) mixture.

- Add the passatta and cook until hot - this removes the uncooked tomato flavour.

- Add the cream and stir well, allowing to cook briefly.

- Add pepper to taste and stir into the pasta.

A nice Italian red would go well with this!

Mike Allen

ROGER ROYLE'S SPINACH PANCAKES.

Serves 4.

First you have to make 12 pancakes*. Well, there is no need for me to tell you how to do those but I shall tell you about the filling.

Ingredients:

>1lb (450 g) fresh spinach or a 1x 12oz (350g) pack of frozen spinach.
>
>1 1/2 oz (40g) butter
>
>1 1/2 oz (40g) flour
>
>I pint (600ml) milk
>
>Salt
>
>Freshly milled pepper
>
>4oz (100g) Gruyere cheese, grated.

Method:

Pre-heat the oven to 400 F (200 C), gas mark 6. If you have a fan oven goodness only knows what you do!

Have your pancakes prepared and hot. If you are using fresh spinach, wash it well and remove the rib from the leaves. I'm lazy – I always use frozen spinach.

Cook in a covered saucepan over a moderate heat for about 10 to 15 minutes, without adding water. Drain well and chop finely. If you are using frozen spinach then follow the instructions on the pack.

Melt the butter in the saucepan over a low heat and stir in the flour. Do this very thoroughly otherwise you get lumps.

Cook gently for a moment, then gradually stir in half the milk, beating well all the time so as to make a thick sauce. Once again keep an eye open for lumps.

Bring to the boil and cook gently for 2 to 3 minutes.

Season with salt and pepper and stir in all but 1oz (25g) of the cheese. Stir about half this sauce into the spinach puree.

Fill the pancakes with the mixture, roll up and place in a buttered serving dish.

Thin down the remaining sauce with the rest of the milk to make a coating consistency. Check the seasoning again and then pour the sauce over the pancakes.

Sprinkle with the remaining cheese and brown well in a hot oven for about 10 minutes.

Serve hot. You can't go wrong.

Canon Roger Royle

*If you *don't* know how to make pancakes, refer to Edi's recipe on page 73.

ENA'S STOVE-TOP WINTER WARMER

Ingredients:

1 tbsp vegetable oil	1 tbsp Worcestershire sauce
1 large onion (chopped)	1 tbsp tomato puree
2 carrots (chopped finely)	1 can chopped tomatoes
1 clove garlic (chopped finely)	1 pint vegetable stock
1 can black-eye beans	1 can red kidney beans
1 can borlotti or canellini beans	1 small can butter beans (optional)

all these beans must be rinsed and drained

Stock can be made using a cube

Dumplings or crusty bread to serve.

Method:

- Heat oil in a large saucepan

- Fry onions, carrots and garlic on a low heat for 10 mins. until carrots tender and onions transparent, but not browned

- Be sure to rinse all the beans thoroughly, and drain before adding to pan, then add all remaining ingredients to the pan and mix well.

- Bring the mixture to the boil on the stove top, and reduce to a simmer for 15 - 20 mins.

(If adding dumplings, place these on top of pan for the last 15 minutes or so of cooking time)

Ena Quandry

MASOOR DERRY DAL

Ingredients:

1/2 lb red lentils	Water as needed
2 Tbsp olive oil	1 Medium onion, thinly sliced
4 Garlic cloves, minced	4 tspn whole coriander seeds
2 tspn cumin seeds	2 tspn cardamom seeds6
2 tspn turmeric powder	4 tspn desiccated coconut
1 Tbsp tamarind paste	6 Tbsp low fat yoghurt
2 tspn hot smoked paprika powder	
6 Inches cinnamon sticks, broken	

Method:

- Wash the lentils well, and then put them into a saucepan. Add 4 - 6 cups of salted water to cover the lentils.

- Bring lentils to a boil then reduce heat, cover and simmer until they are soft. Keep the water level above the lentils.

- While the lentils are simmering, grind the spices together then toast them over low heat in a dry sauté pan until you have released their aromas. Set spices aside.

- Using the same sauté pan, heat ghee or oil over low to medium heat. Sauté onions until soft. Add garlic and sauté another 3-4 minutes. Do not burn the onions or garlic. Add spice mixture; continue to cook for 2 minutes.

- Add lentils and their cooking liquid to the onion and spice mixture (add more water or broth if lentil are too thick). Stir and scrape up any bit from the bottom. Stir in tamarind, adjust salt and continue to cook for 5 minutes.

- Just before serving add yoghurt and coconut and heat through.

Cara Van Parc

HOT CHILLI CHUTNEY

Ingredients:

    6 sweet apples, chopped   4 potatoes, chopped

    2 large onions, chopped,   1 bulb of garlic, sliced small

    1 pint malt vinegar   1 lb of granulated sugar

    Drop of oil   Basil, shredded

    Glug of tomato sauce   Teaspoon of pickling spice

    1 whole lemon, chopped (skin, pith etc)

Mix all ingredients together and add 24 red chillies, chopped

Made 5 jars

Graham Dunbar

MUM'S MARROW POT

Ingredients:

    One marrow, peeled, deseeded & cut into chunks about 2" x 1"

    Sliced tomatoes   Sliced Onions   Butter

Method:

- Grease an ovenproof dish with butter
- Layer the onion in the bottom of the dish, then the marrow and then tomatoes.
- Put a few knobs of butter on the top then cover with foil and seal.
- Cook in a moderately slow oven for about 40 mins

Rhea Juvenate

CAROL'S COLESLAW - HOLD THE MAYO

Ingredients:

For the Dressing:

    1 capful of olive oil

    4 capfuls of balsamic vinegar

    Ground mixed cracked pepper & chilli flakes to taste

For the Coleslaw:

    1 small beetroot

    1 jerusalem artichoke

    1 carrot   } All raw and grated

    Some nice swede

    Some nice red cabbage

    Some nice onion

Method:

- Mix the veg with the dressing.
- Leave to marinade a little and eat.

Really nice and low fat!

You can add a handful of organic drained and rinsed chickpeas if you want a bit of protein

Carol Dickens

'Chunky Sauce'
to go with spare ribs or grilled belly pork.

Ingredients:

    1 small tin Cream of Tomato soup

    1 small tin pineapple slices or chunks

    1 apple

    1 medium onion

    1 green pepper

    2 tbsp dark soy sauce

    1 tsp hot chilli powder or more to taste if desired.

Method:

- Strain pineapple and reserve juice
- Chop pineapple, onion, pepper and apple fairly fine
- Put soup into a saucepan and add chopped vegetables, soy sauce and chilli, stir well and heat gently till just simmering
- Add pineapple juice if you wish to thin sauce and add flavour.

Pour over grilled ribs or belly; serve with rice or noodles, or crusty bread to mop up.

Pam Bloodworth

PANCAKE BATTER

These amounts should make 12 x 8" diameter thin pancakes, just right for Canon Roger Royle's "Spinach Pancakes" recipe.

Ingredients:

    200g plain flour   oil for frying

    2 eggs   500ml skimmed or semi-skimmed milk

Method:

- Sieve flour into mixing bowl. Make a well in the centre.
- Break eggs into well and add 4 tbsp of the milk.
- With a wooden spoon or spatula gradually mix so that flour starts to blend in.
- As mixture thickens add more milk, a little at a time, and mix slowly so no lumps form, until all milk is added and all flour is mixed in.
- Beat until smooth. (If you do happen to get lumps you can put the batter into a blender and whizz it around a bit!!)
- Pour into a jug. Lightly brush base of 8"/20cm frying pan (or crepe pan if you have one) with oil.
- Heat oil and pour in 2 or 3 tbsp batter---enough to evenly and thinly coat base of pan.
- Cook until golden brown and then, if you're brave enough, toss pancake. If you think you might finish up with it on the ceiling perhaps it would be better to turn it over with a fish slice!!!
- Cook second side until golden and mottled.
- Repeat with rest of mixture until you have a stack of pancakes.

**Pancakes can be made in advance and stored in 'fridge in an airtight container, with greaseproof paper between each pancake, for 1 or 2 days.

Edina Cloud

FRUIT AND NUT SALAD

Serves 4

Ingredients:

    1 Banana chopped

    2 medium Apples thickly sliced

    1 handful Pine nuts

    2 Tomatoes chopped

    2 sticks of Celery chopped

    1 Cucumber diced

    Half of a red/green/orange or yellow Pepper sliced

    1 dessertspoon dollop salad cream

    1 dessertspoon dollop mayonnaise

Method:

- Combine everything except the pine nuts into a salad bowl adding the two dollops last and gently mix to cover evenly.
- Sprinkle the pine nuts over the top

Gavin Murrell

GINGER AND ORANGE PUD

Ingredients:

    1 Jamaica Ginger Cake sliced

    1 tin mandarin oranges drained
    (set a few segments aside for decoration)

    1/2 pt double cream - whipped

Method:

- Layer the oranges and ginger cake slices starting and finishing with cake.
- Pour over the juice and leave for 10 minutes.
- Cover with cream and decorate with the reserved segments.
- Serve

Jane Minto

HAWAIIAN SALAD

Ingredients:

2 cups of chopped marshmallows	1 cup desiccated coconut
1 cup of chopped pineapple (fresh or tinned in juice, drained)	1 cup of mandarin oranges (tinned in juice, drained)

    1 large tub of soured cream.

Method:

Mix all ingredients together and preferably leave overnight before serving.

Kay Davie

JO'S ALMOND SLICE

This is a Swedish tray bake, which is called "Mazarin Rutor".

My sister and I loved messing in the kitchen when we were young and this was one of our favorites.

It is easy to do and keeps for a good week on the counter if well wrapped. Mind you, in our house we rarely managed to keep it that long.

It is also a brilliant cake to keep handy in the freezer for those unexpected guests. Freeze it without the icing of course!

Ingredients:

Sponge mix:

- 200g Butter
- 2 Eggs
- 2 tsp Vanilla Essence
- 350 ml Plain Flour
- 1 tsp Baking Powder
- 150 ml Milk
- 300 ml Caster Sugar
- ½ tsp Almond Essence
- 50g Ground Almonds

Icing:

- 300g Icing Sugar
- 4 Tbsp Water or Orange Juice

Method:

- Preheat oven gas mark 3 / 175C/ Fan 150C
- Grease a deep baking dish (I use a normal Pyrex dish measuring 20cm x 30cm) and dust some dry ground breadcrumbs or plain flour and shake off excess.
- Melt the butter and take off the heat and cool by adding the milk.

- With an electric beater, whip up the egg and sugar until pale and fluffy. It will only take a few minutes.

- Then stir in the butter, milk and the two essences. Finally, sift in all the dry ingredients, fold in and pour into the baking tray.

- Bake until dark golden brown and a skewer will come out clean. (app 40 mins)

- Leave it to cool down before spreading the icing.

- To make the icing - sift the icing sugar and whisk in the liquid until smooth.

- Now you can either turn it over onto a serving plate and ice it upside down or simply leave it in the dish and cut a piece as you need it. Drizzle the icing over the top and spread it gently.

Wait until icing is set before cutting.

Jo – The Bruntonside

SIMPLE DESSERT

Mix fresh fruit in dessert bowl.

My fave is raspberries, blueberries and chopped strawberries.
Pour over natural yoghurt and sprinkle with muesli. I can recommend Dorset Cereals Fruit, Nuts & seeds.

Dead easy, and it makes a lovely fresh breakfast dish as well.

Lucy Quipment

FRUIT CHEESECAKE

Ingredients:

- 1 fruit jelly
- ¼ pt hot water
- 8oz cottage cheese
- 5oz double cream
- 6oz digestive biscuits or chocolate digestive
- 3oz melted butter

Method:

- Crush biscuits and mix with melted butter.
- Cover base of 7 or 8 inch loose bottom cake tin or flan dish deep enough to take cheesecake mixture.
- Put in fridge until ready to pour over cheese mixture.
- Dissolve jelly in hot water; allow to cool but not to set.
- Put cottage cheese in blender gradually adding cream; blitz till smooth then add jelly (gradually pour into blender).
- Then pour over biscuit base. Leave to set in fridge. When set decorate with fruit.
- Can be frozen. Wrap in tinfoil once it has frozen then put in either plastic box or bag. Will keep for up to a month.

Just change the flavour of jelly to whatever fruit you use i.e. strawberry/mandarins/raspberry.

You can add a layer of fruit to the biscuit base before pouring filling over.

Jacqueline Page

LEMON CHEESECAKE

Ingredients:

Base

    8oz digestive biscuits (crushed)

    4oz butter   1oz demerara sugar

Filling

    ½ lemon jelly dissolved in 3 tbsp water

    juice of one lemon   small tin carnation milk

    3oz philadelphia cheese   3oz caster sugar

    small carton double cream

Method:

Base

- Melt butter then add biscuit and sugar
- Mix together then put into a flan dish and press down firmly.
- Put in fridge to chill

Filling

- Dissolve jelly in water, let cool (not set)
- Whip carnation milk and lemon juice until thick
- In another bowl beat caster sugar and cheese together
- Then gently spoon in the carnation milk and lemon juice
- Whisk double cream a little then add to rest of mixture
- Spread on top of biscuit base chill for a couple of hours

Tricia Hudson (Big T)

LEMON FREEZE

Ingredients:

For the base

    3oz crushed cornflakes (or Frosties, or whatever you've got!)

    3oz castor sugar (optional)

    3oz melted butter

For the topping

    2 eggs   1 small can condensed milk

    1oz castor sugar   ¼ pint of double cream

    2 lemons, grated and squeezed

Method:

- Make base -mix together all the ingredients and press into base of a greased dish -and leave to chill.
- Separate eggs – add the yolks, condensed milk, and cream together and blend well.
- Add lemon juice and grated rind and stir into mixture till it thickens.
- Beat egg whites until stiff, and then stir in sugar until glossy.
- Fold egg whites into lemon mixture and pour over base.
- Freeze immediately, and then decorate when you take it out to serve.

Best taken out of freezer when you start the main course, otherwise its too hard.

Janet & John Marsh

LEMON BRIOCHE PUDDING

Ingredients:

- 2 x Brioche plait loaves
- 1½ pints single cream
- ½ pint full fat milk
- 7 eggs
- 1 lemon
- 2 jars lemon curd
- 1 pkt unsalted butter

Method:

- Butter a large dish.
- Slice loaves, spread butter on one side and lemon curd on the other.
- Layer them in the dish with the lemon curd side on top.
- All this can be done in advance and covered with cling film.
- Mix together eggs, milk and cream, and leave to stand for 1 hour.
- Pour over bread, together with the juice and rind of the lemon.
- Try to avoid having the crusts on top.
- Bake for 20 mins at 200°C or Gas Mark 6.

This is a delicious and rich pudding!

Sally Boazman

ORANGE WHIP

Ingredients:

1 tin mandarin oranges, in juice	25g cornflour
25g caster sugar	2 eggs
1 lemon	25g margarine

Method:

- Drain juice from oranges into measuring jug. Add enough water to reach 250ml mark.
- Chop oranges, leaving 8 neat segments for decoration.
- Place cornflour in small pan and add 6 tbsp of the liquid from the jug.
- Using a wooden spoon blend the cornflour and liquid together until smooth. Add rest of liquid and caster sugar.
- Finely grate zest from lemon and add to pan.
- Separate eggs, placing whites into a mixing bowl and yolks into pan.
- Place pan on low heat and stir all the time with wooden spoon until mixture bubbles and thickens.
- Remove from heat. Add lemon juice, chopped fruit and margarine. Mix well.
- Whisk egg white until stiff. Using a tablespoon gently fold orange mixture into egg whites.
- Pile into serving dishes and decorate with orange segments.

Can sprinkle with chocolate bits too if you like - a dark flake works wonders!!!

Har Monica

HELLEN'S PINK FLUFFY THING

Ingredients:

½ pint double cream (for whipping purposes)

1 punnet raspberries or strawberries

6 tsp Splenda

Very thin, very dark chocolate pieces – the thinner and darker the better

Method:

- Put fruit in a bowl and add sweet stuff (Splenda or sugar)
- Mash with potato masher according to lumpiness preferences
- In a separate bowl whisk cream until light and fluffy
- Fold mashed fruit into the bowl of fluffiness
- Chill for at least 1 hour
- When serving sprinkle chocolate pieces over the top
- Enjoy!

Hellen Bach

Editor's note – other sweeteners are available

AMERICAN NUT WONDER

Ingredients:

    6 oz shortbread finger biscuits, crushed
    (Put in plastic bag & crush with rolling pin)

    3 oz crushed walnuts

    5 oz icing sugar

    4 oz butter

    2 eggs

    1 large tin crushed pineapple, drained (but save the juice)

    ¼ - ½ pint whipping cream

Method:

- Line base of glass dish with biscuit crumbs (reserving a few to sprinkle on top of dessert to finish)
- Cream together icing sugar, butter & eggs, to form a smooth custard. Spread evenly on top of crumbs.
- Then add layer of crushed walnuts, followed by a layer of crushed pineapple.
- Whisk cream & spread it on top, finishing with a light sprinkling of biscuit crumbs.
- Serve with pouring cream & the pineapple juice.

It is more-ish....... but providing you eat it in the dark, or out of someone else's dish, it has no calories!!

Elaine Cohen-Dorff

BAD KING HEROD'S PUDDING

Ingredients:

    8 oz brown bread breadcrumbs   1 tbsp cocoa

    4 oz demerara sugar   500 ml double cream

100 ml juice - this can be pure orange juice or you can (and I recommend you do) add in a significant shot of tia maria; cointreau or baileys or to be honest whatever takes your fancy) - look we are togs we might need different measures!!

selection of fruit - grapes, strawberries and pineapple chunks are great - just see which is most beyond its sell by date. If you use tinned fruit, use the juice as part of your 100ml

This will make enough for a small dessert bowl, just scale up the quantities for larger bowls

Method:

- Mix the breadcrumbs, sugar and cocoa together
- Whisk the cream until it is coming into soft peaks. Do not let it get too stiff, if you do, loosen it with some juice
- Build up layers of crumb, a small amount of the fruit in the bowl and cream - pour a little of the juice as you make each layer but try and have about 50 ml juice left at the end. I usually just do 2 thick layers but you can do 3 thinner layers
- Finish with a layer of crumb and a decorative layer of fruit
- Pour the remaining liquid over so it soaks through
- Cover with clingfilm and refrigerate it for at least 6 hours

The result will be a lovely chocolatey, gooey trifle type pudding

Sometimes I add chocolate shavings in the layers

Old Mrs J

VERY RICH CHOCOLATE MOUSSE

Ingredients:

You will need per person:-

    A small wine glass or small coffee cup and saucer

    1 free range egg and 2 oz of Bourneville chocolate (I have tried others but this works best)

    Plus 1 extra egg white (I find this makes for a slightly softer mousse)

    To decorate you need softly whipped double cream and a little grated chocolate

    Sponge fingers or ratafia biscuits are a nice accompaniment

Method:

- Separate the egg yolks from the whites, put whites into a really clean large bowl ready to whip them.

- Break the chocolate up into squares and either melt them in a microwave or over a pan of boiling water. Be careful not to overheat or get water in with the chocolate.

- Whilst the chocolate is melting whisk the egg whites till they are very stiff.

- Let the chocolate cool a little before you add the beaten egg yolks. If you add them when it is too hot you will end up with chocolate scrambled eggs! The mixture will thicken a little.

- Add a large spoonful of the whites to the chocolate mixture and mix well, to slacken the mix. Then add all the chocolate mix to the whites and mix until it is a uniform colour. Spoon carefully in to your chosen serving dish and leave a small gap at the top. Chill.

- Before serving cover the top of the chocolate mousse completely with the lightly whipped cream and dust with grated chocolate. It tastes even better if made the day before!

Penny Jennings

IRISH WHISKEY SYLLABUB
A quick, delicious dessert in honour of Sir Terry.

Ingredients:

250ml double cream	1 lemon
5 tbsp clear honey	6 tbsp Irish malt whiskey

Method:

- Grate rind from lemon and squeeze juice. Put in mixing bowl with whiskey and honey and leave to stand - overnight if possible - so flavours develop.
- Whisk in the cream gradually until mixture starts to thicken.
- Spoon into wine glasses and serve immediately, or leave in fridge until needed.

If left to stand it separates into 2 layers--thick and creamy topping with a clear liquid at the bottom

Victoria Plum

IT CAN HAPPEN TO THE BEST OF COOKS: DISASTER PUDDING!

I like to pride myself on my cooking and baking ability. I think of myself as a good cook, able to make up recipes using my cookery knowledge. However, be warned; things can go wrong, horribly wrong … *scary laugh of doom*

Ingredients:

    1 packet of jelly – any flavour it's all going to go wrong anyway
    About 10 sponge fingers   Large measure of gin

Method:

- Have a happy and cheerful outlook and make up the packet of jelly in a large bowl.
- Happily take the sponge fingers WITHOUT soaking them in anything like liqueur or syrup and carefully dunk the sponge fingers into the jelly.
- Wait patiently for the sponge fingers to sink lower into the jelly smiling all the while … keep waiting … and waiting … and waiting …
- Wonder what to do and get slightly concerned. A furrowed brow is optional.
- Still waiting … and waiting…
- Taking a wooden spoon gentle prod the sponge fingers to make them sink into the jelly mixture.
- Watch in annoyance as they bob to the top.
- Prod with the wooden spoon again, this time more vigorously.
- Swear loudly as sponge fingers refuse to play fair and rise to the top again.
- Drink large measure of gin, and when serving the disaster pudding say 'it is meant to be like that' and roll your eyes when questioned!

Tigger

MUVVER'S EASY ICE CREAM

This is my easiest-any-dam-fool-can make-it Ice cream recipe from my Mum

Ingredients:

    One 500ml carton of whipping cream

    One 400 ml tin of condensed milk

Method:

- Whip the cream until thick
- Gradually add the can of condensed milk so the mix remains thick and thickens even more
- Bung into a plastic container and place in freezer for a couple of hours
- Lick spoon
- Wait by the freezer for aaaaages but do NOT poke it because that means you have to wait even longer!

This is the vanilla version. We have added the following flavours to vary it

Two table spoons Irish Cream Liqueur

Some fresh, mashed, raspberries or strawberries

Melted Cadbury Dairy Milk

Half a jar of toffee sauce (most of it got stuck on the spoon and licked off)

MuvverSoup
Mother Superior of the Convent of the Sisters of Perpetual PMT

FRUIT CRUMBLE

Ingredients:

Either 4-5 large fresh apples (or pears, same volume of blackberries etc.), OR two tins of prepared apples in own juice or light syrup (or pears, or peaches etc.)

150g wholemeal plain flour

50g caster sugar for the crumble mixture

30g sugar if using fresh fruit

50g margarine or butter

1 tsp ground cinnamon (optional)

Method:

- Pre heat the oven to a medium-high heat for 15 minutes.
- If you are using fresh fruit wash it and chop it up into chunks (remove peel if you wish. I like to leave it on when making an apple crumble, but not a pear one).
- Stew the fruit in the microwave with about a cup of water, 30g of sugar, and cinnamon if using. You want the fruit to be soft but not collapsed, so cook for about 5 minutes on high and then check to see if it needs more cooking.
- Pour the cooked fruit or tinned fruit into the base of a shallow baking dish.
- To make up the crumble mixture simply rub in the rest of the fat with the flour in a bowl using the rubbing in method, ie until the mixture resembles bread crumbs.
- Add the sugar to the crumble mixture and then spoon it on top of the fruit. This doesn't have to be perfect.

- Bake on top shelf the oven with a foil cover for about 15-20 minutes, and for the last 5-10 minutes leave the foil cover off.
- The crumble is ready to eat on its own or you can add a dollop of ice cream, custard, or yoghurt.

Tigger

WONDERFUL ICE CREAM

Ingredients:

    4 eggs

    4oz icing sugar

    ½ pint double cream

    4 dssp dandelion coffee granules

    1 dssp hot water.

Method:

- Dissolve the coffee in the water.
- Separate the eggs
- Whip the whites until stiff
- Add the sugar and the coffee to the cream, and whip until thick but not hard.
- Blend the cream and egg yolks thoroughly with the egg whites.
- Pour into a container and freeze, stirring once or twice during freezing (about 3-4 hours).

I call this 'Wonderful Ice-cream' as many people have a prejudice against dandelion coffee; anyone who has tasted it agrees with the name.

Valerie McMillan

PUD WITH NO NAME

Serves up to 8, depending on appetite (the use of butter makes for a richer taste, and the use of cooking or eating apples is a matter for your taste buds)!

Pudding

Ingredients:

    8 ozs (227g) self-raising flour

    2 ozs (57g) margarine or butter

    1 lb (454g) cooking or eating apples (weight BEFORE peeling and coring; this is just 3 or 4 standard-sized apples)

Method:

- Rub the flour and margarine (or butter) together, then mix with water until it is a soft dough. Roll out into a 12" (30.5 cm) round.

- Peel, core, and thinly slice the apples. Pile into the middle of the dough, then fold over and seal the edges into a neat parcel.

- Place into a 2½ pint (1.5 l) casserole dish, making sure that the sealed edges are on the bottom of the dish.

Sauce

Ingredients:

    2 ozs (57g) margarine or butter

    ½ pint (284ml) water

    8 ozs (227g) brown sugar (the darker the sugar, the darker the sauce)

Method:

- Put all the ingredients into a saucepan, heating until the butter and sugar have dissolved, then pour carefully around the pudding (NOT over the top).

- Do not cover the dish.

- Cook at 190ºC (375ºF / gas mark 5) for 40-45 minutes until golden brown.

- Serve immediately.

TIP: If you make 1½ or 2 times the amount of sauce, reserve the extra to use as a pour-on sauce when serving.

Bea Sotted

BRANDY PUDDING

Ingredients:

PUDDING

250g stoned dates, diced	1 cup boiling water *
1 tspn bicarbonate of soda	100g butter, at room temp
1 cup castor sugar	1 large egg, at room temp
1¼ cups flour	pinch of salt
½ tspn baking powder	1¼ cups chopped pecans

SAUCE

¾ cup sugar	¾ cup water
1 Tbsp butter	1 tspn vanilla extract
½ cup brandy **	

Method:

To Make Tart

- Sprinkle bicarbonate of soda over the dates and pour the boiling water over them. Leave to cool.
- Cream the butter and sugar in a mixing bowl.
- When the butter mixture is light and creamy, gradually beat in the egg.
- Sift the dry ingredients and fold them and the dates into the creamed mixture, using a metal spoon.
- If putting pecans into the pudding, add them now as well, keeping some back for decoration.
- Pour mixture into a greased 25 cm pie dish or cake tin. I use a deep 10" loose-bottom cake tin - it rises more than you think.

- Bake at 180 C (350 F) for 45 minutes until dark brown and done.

To Make Sauce

- Bring the sugar, water and butter to the boil, remove from the heat and add the vanilla and brandy.
- Pour the warm sauce over the hot cake and leave in the tin to cool. It looks WAY too much sauce, but it really soaks in.

Cut the tart into portions. Top with fresh cream (piped in pretty curls if you want) and a sprinkling of chopped pecan nuts.

It can be served as a cake, but beware - it's very moist and gooey!

* For anyone worried about cup measurements, get a set of measuring cups and use those,. Just don't mix and match!"

** I've been told you could use sherry, or even orange juice, but I've never got past the brandy!!

LUCY QUIPMENT

APPLE SNOW

My family's favourite dessert. My youngest son gave it its name as it looks like snow when mixed.

Ingredients:

    250g cooking apples

    2 tspn lemon juice

    2 tbsp sugar - to go in pan with apples

    100ml milk   2 tspn sugar - to go in sauce

    1 egg   2 trifle sponges

    decoration eg chocolate sprinkles, chopped nuts, glace cherries

Method:

- Peel, core and chop apples. Stew in medium pan with lemon juice and sugar until soft. Leave to cool.
- Break up sponges and place in base of trifle dish or individual dishes.
- Separate egg. Put white in a small bowl.
- Put egg yolk in small pan with milk and sugar. Cook over gentle heat stirring all the time with a wooden spoon until mixture starts to thicken and coats the back of the spoon. (Don't let it overcook or it goes like scrambled egg).
- Pour evenly over sponges.
- Whisk egg white until stiff and fold into apples.
- Pile on top of sponge and decorate.

Victoria Plum

Cheat's Lemon Meringue

Ingredients:

Double cream - Quantity will depend upon size of a) Base and b) Appetite.

Lemon Curd (preferably home made - as in from your local WI Market) 1 Jar

Meringue Base (yes you've guessed it - from your local WI Market)

Method:

- Queue patiently to enter your WI market - please try to ignore those delightful little old ladies who seem not to see you standing there. Buy meringue base and 'Home Made' lemon curd.
- Whip double cream until firm. Stir in sufficient Lemon Curd to the cream to fill the meringue base.
- Fill base of meringue with mixture
- Place in fridge until required.
- Lick spoon and sit back to await the complimentary comments at your achievement.

Carl Ott

Cheats Caramel Tart

Ingredients:

    Double Cream (do you see a pattern developing?)

    Dark brown Muscovado sugar

    Pie base from your local Tesbags outlet

Method:

(Prepare a few hours ahead of serving).

- Whip double cream until firm.
- Fold in sugar and set aside to allow the flavours and colour of the sugar to permeate the cream until an even brown all over.
- Fill pie base with the mixture and make pretty swirly pattern with the back of a fork.
- Place in fridge until required.

Carl Ott

FRIDGE CAKE

Ingredients:

4oz Butter Unsalted	6oz Chocolate
2oz Raisins	2oz Walnuts
4 Tbsp of Brandy	¼ Pint Double Cream
2 Eggs	8oz Plain Marie Biscuits (or Rich Tea biscuits if not available)

Method:

- Crush up the biscuits with a rolling pin (to a large crumb),
- Melt the Butter and chocolate, and stir together until fully mixed
- Pour the butter and chocolate mix over the biscuits,
- Then add all of the remaining ingredients and stir until well mixed,
- Line a 2 pound loaf tin with greaseproof paper, leaving an inch or 2 over the edges all round
- Put the mixture into the loaf tin,
- Place the loaf tin into the refrigerator for 3 or 4 hours
- Remove, cut into portions and enjoy !!!
- For an extra rich treat, try serving it cold and covered with double cream

Robin Winterton

BREAD AND BUTTER PUDDING
serves 4

Ingredients:

8 slices of slightly stale, buttered bread (white or brown).

2oz Sultanas – soaked in Rum

Grated rind of ½ a lemon.

2 Eggs

3 level Tbsp caster sugar.

1 pt of vanilla flavoured milk
(use fresh vanilla pod or vanilla essence)

Method:

- Preheat oven to Gas Mark 4 / 350 F/ 180 C
- Remove the crusts from the buttered bread and cut into 4 squares (or triangles) per slice.
- Place them in a buttered oven dish with alternate layers of sultanas and lemon rind.
- Beat the eggs lightly with 2 Tbsp of the sugar and add the milk. Pour this mix over the bread
- Sprinkle the remaining sugar over the top and bake for about 30 mins or until lightly browned.
- Serve with Custard, Cream or Ice Cream.

Tip – if you have any Rum left over, add it to the milk mix – yummy.

Hugh Cookson

RECIPE FOR DISASTER

Loose Women

Beer

Hugh Cookson

TOG PANCAKE MIXTURE
A Special Occasion Treat

In case you are wondering what to do for dinner and you are stuck on what to cook for a special person, it is all sorted!

Ingredients:

    Large quantities of your dinner guest's favourite flower

    A huge pinch of salt

    A couple of yolks

    Milk it, for what it is worth

    Plenty of buttering up

Method:

- Gently heat the butter
- Beat all the other ingredients together (the whip should only be used when one is trying to lighten up)
- Fry in the butter until the batter stiffens
- Depending on your how familiar you are with your dinner party guest you may be permitted to flip every now and again
- Serve with a smile.

Poppy Cock

EARLY MORNING PICK UP

A good measure of Wake up to Wogan

Mixed with Janet & John Stories

Then add: -

A large spoonful of forgetfulness

A bucket of laughter

Mix together with a collection of very odd names

Special ingredients to be added when required

A cupful of Deadly Alancoat

Two spoonfuls of Charlie Nove

Some Boggy Marsh to taste

To be taken regularly every week-day morning

At 7.30 am as the best start to the day.

Jean Savill

TOGS' HOME FOR THE BEWILDERED

Ingredients:

For the building:-

    300g S R flour

    2 level tspn baking powder

    240g soft tub margarine

    240g caster sugar

    4 eggs

    1 packet ready rolled white icing

For roof, windows, doors, chimney, garden and anything else:-

    Coloured icing blocks - can get 4 colours in a packet

    Icing pens of various colours

    Jam

Method:

- Sieve flour and baking powder into large mixing bowl.
- Add sugar, margarine and eggs and mix thoroughly with electric mixer - or wooden spoon if you're feeling energetic - until you get a soft creamy consistency.
- Divide evenly into 2 non-stick (or 2 greased and lined) 8" square tins.
- Bake at Gas 4 or 180C for 25 minutes or until firm and shrinking from sides of tins.
- Turn out onto cooling rack.

- When cake is cool cut one in half and the other one into 3 even pieces.
- Spread a little jam on the halves and put together to form base of house.
- Use two of the smaller pieces on top, again using jam to stick them together.
- Cover with ready rolled white icing and mould into shape to form walls. Trim edges.
- Roll out trimmings to cover a small piece of remaining cake for the chimney.
- Roll out one piece of coloured icing and cut into small squares----we used red---and overlap these to make roof.
- Roll out other colours for rest of decoration on house and surroundings, and use icing pens for the fiddly bits.

It helps if you get a gang of Togs on the project, each using imagination and artistic skills to complete the task!!

TLA – Elite Regiment

LYNN BOWLES' CHOCOLATE CAKE

Ingredients:

- 85g good quality plain chocolate
- 225g unsalted butter
- 325g plain flour
- ½ tspn salt
- 150ml boiling water
- 3 eggs
- 350g dark brown sugar
- 2 tspn bicarbonate of soda
- 115ml buttermilk
- 2 tspn vanilla extract

for the glaze

- 175g good quality plain chocolate
- pinch of salt
- 75g icing sugar
- 75g unsalted butter

Method:

- Preheat oven 180 C / 350 F / Gas mark 4
- Grease and flour a 25cm cake tin with 5cm high sides
- Break up chocolate in a bowl, melt over pan of boiling water (or in microwave)
- Cream together butter and brown sugar until fluffy
- Beat the eggs and add gradually, whisking well between each addition
- Stir in melted chocolate
- Sieve flour, bicarbonate and salt and fold in along with buttermilk
- Slowly add boiling water stirring well to combine
- Add vanilla extract, pour into tin and bake for 45 – 50 mins, or until skewer inserted in the middle comes out clean. Allow cake to cool in the tin
- Place ingredients for glaze in a bowl over pan of simmering water. Heat and stir gently until mixture is smooth
- Ice the cake while the glaze is still warm, it will set when cool

LYNN BOWLES

ECONOMICAL CHOCOLATE CAKE

Ingredients:

- ½ lb self raising flour
- 2 ozs margarine
- 1 level Tbsp cocoa
- 1 dessertspoon treacle
- 1 tspn bicarbonate of soda
- 3 ozs granulated sugar
- 11 Tbsp hot water

Method:

- Put sugar, treacle and margarine in a mixing bowl and add most of the water, mix and allow to cool.
- Sift the flour and cocoa together and then add to the mixture.
- Dissolve the bicarb of soda in the remaining hot water and mix all together.
- Grease two 7" sandwich tins and divide the mixture equally.
- Bake for 15 minutes at 450/230 gas mark 8.
- When cooled sandwich together with fresh whipped cream or butter cream and add a layer of strawberry jam if the granchildren are coming.

Molly Coddle

7 MINUTE CHOCOLATE CAKE

There is no weighing involved here, all you need for this cake is a measuring jug as all measurements are in mls NOT gms. This is quick and easy with a capital Q and a capital E. The cake stays moist and delish for a week at least, if it lasts that long.

Ingredients:

- 250ml plain flour
- 15ml baking powder
- 125ml melted butter
- 2 large eggs
- 1 slab chocolate (melted over pan of hot water)
- 60ml cocoa powder
- 250ml caster sugar
- 125ml brewed coffee (cooled)
- 125ml cream

Method:

- Sift together flour, cocoa powder, baking powder and castor sugar
- Gently whisk melted butter, coffee and eggs
- Mix wet and dry together and pour into a greased 2 litre ice cream container (to grease, rub butter all over container and dust with cocoa powder). Ensure container is microwaveable.
- Place an inverted saucer or bowl in microwave, place cake container on top and microwave for 7 minutes on high.
- For the topping – mix together the cream and melted chocolate
- When cake is cool lather on the topping.(You can have more fun at this stage by sprinkling over some coarsely chopped Ferrero Rocher or other chocolate/biscuit type bar.)

Hilary Farrell

APPLE CAKE

Ingredients:

    12oz SR Flour

    8oz Butter

    6oz Caster sugar

    4oz Sultanas (you can use mixed fruit)

    3 eggs lightly beaten

    1lb cooking apples or ¾lb gooseberries

Method:

- Preheat oven Gas Mark 4 / 180c
- Rub butter and flour together to make breadcrumb like texture
- Peel/core and slice apples
- Stir all the dry ingredients together with the sliced apples
- Add eggs and mix
- Put into 8" cake tin or 2 loaf tins lined with greaseproof or non-stick baking parchment and bake for 1¼ hours or until firm to the touch.
- Leave to cool in tin

Jacqueline Page

RABBI PETE'S HONEY CAKE
FOR ROSH HASHANAH (JEWISH NEW YEAR)

Ingredients:

- 2 tbsp Golden Syrup
- 2 eggs
- half cup white sugar
- 1 tspn bicarbonate soda
- 1 tspn mixed spice
- flaked almonds for the top
- 3 cups self-raising flour (sieved)
- 2 tbsp runny honey
- 1 cup dark brown sugar
- 1 cup strong black coffee
- 1 tspn baking powder
- 1 cup vegetable oil

Method:

- Preheat oven Gas mark 4, (350F, 180C)
- Line and grease a cake tin
- Mix all ingredients together until smooth
- Pour into cake tin
- Sprinkle top with flaked almonds
- Cook for 1-1¼ hours
- Turn out onto cooling rack

Enjoy!

RABBI PETE TOBIAS

ROBBIE TOBIAS' HONEY CAKE

Ingredients:

250g clear honey

100g dark muscovado sugar

300g self-raising flour

Handful of flaked almonds for top

225g unsalted butter

3 large eggs, beaten

Method:

- Preheat the oven to fan 140C/ conventional 160C/gas 3. Butter and line a 20cm cake tin.

- Cut the butter into pieces and drop into a medium pan with the honey and sugar. Melt slowly over a low heat. When the mixture looks quite liquid, increase the heat under the pan and boil for about one minute. Leave to cool for about 30 minutes, to prevent the eggs cooking when they are mixed in.

- Beat the eggs into the melted honey mixture using a wooden spoon. Sift the flour into a large bowl and pour in the egg and honey mixture, beating until smooth and runny.

- Pour the mixture into the tin and sprinkle top with flaked almonds. Bake for 50 minutes -1 hour, until the cake is well-risen, golden brown and springs back when pressed. A skewer pushed into the centre of the cake should come out clean.

- Turn the cake out on a wire rack. Then leave to cool.

Robbie Tobias
wife of Rabbi Pete

COFFEE INDEMORN CUP CAKES

Makes about 12 big cupcakes

INGREDIENTS:

For the cup cakes :

    400g tin of plum tomatoes - whole or chopped (*optional*) *

4 oz butter	4 oz soft light brown sugar
4 oz self-raising flour	2 eggs
2 tbsp cream	½ tsp baking powder
1 tbsp good quality instant coffee *nothing wishy-washy*	1 tbsp boiling water to dissolve the coffee in

For the icing:

12 oz of sifted icing sugar	1 tbsp good quality instant coffee
1 tbsp boiling water to dissolve the coffee in	warm water

    around a dozen large muffin cases

METHOD :

To make the cup cakes :

- Preheat the oven to Gas Mark 5 / 190C / 375F. Put the muffin cases into a muffin tray if you've got one or the deepest bun tray you have. If you don't have a bun tray you can use doubled up muffin cases to hold the cakes more firmly and discard the outer ones before you ice them.

- Dissolve the coffee in the boiling water and leave to cool a little, but not go completely cold.

- Cream together the butter and sugar until it pales in colour - you might want to get one of the staff to do this bit as it can be a bit exhausting.

- One at a time, break the eggs into a small bowl and whisk lightly then add to the mixture, stirring until it is fully combined.

- Sift together the flour and baking powder then add in stages to the mixture, beating until it is fully combined.

- Don't over beat or you'll knock all the air out of the mixture.

- Add the coffee and cream and beat one final time.

- Divide the mixture between the muffin cases filling each one no more than just over half full. Smooth the top if it doesn't smooth itself - it should settle nicely with a flat surface.

- Bake for about 20 minutes. The cup cakes should rise to fill all but about 1/4-1/2" and have a flat surface that springs back when lightly pressed. Cool on a wire rack.

To make the icing :

- There's a degree of adaptation with this because how much icing you need depends on how full the muffin cases are. Ideally, you want a thick layer of icing. Also, personal taste will dictate how strongly flavoured the icing is. If you want it stronger, put in more coffee. There's a degree of trial and error but the ultimate Coffee Indemorn Cup Cake icing will be just solid enough to lift away from the cake complete with pleating from the muffin case and have a surface that flexes and cracks slightly if you poke it.

- Dissolve the coffee in the boiling water. Sift the icing sugar into a bowl and mix in the coffee stirring until it has mixed as well as possible. Then add the warm water a little at a time, stirring vigorously until you get a just pourable, slightly stiff consistency. Do not have it too runny or it won't set.

- Help the icing onto the cupcakes with a small flattish spoon or a spatula and level it off. Get it as close to the top of the cases as possible without it spilling over. Leave to set.

These cup cakes actually taste better if you leave them for 24-48 hours before eating them. The flavour seems to develop and the icing sets with a slightly crunchy surface. I've no idea how long they keep for because they usually last only a day or so at Indemorn Towers!

* the tin of tomatoes is useful for propping the recipe book against while you're making the cup cakes, which prevents mixture getting splattered all over the pages. It can be returned to the pantry afterwards.

Earl Leigh Indemorn

BREAD PUDDING

Ingredients:

    1 x large loaf

    175g/6oz self raising flour

    225g/8oz sugar

    50g mixed spice

    175g/6oz margarine

    350g dried mixed fruit

    Pinch of salt.

Method:

This is a very hands on recipe and works best using your hands only.

- Soak the bread in water for about 10 mins then squeeze out the water.
- Mix the bread and margarine together thoroughly.
- Add all the dry ingredients and mix together.(by hand).
- Add the fruit and mix in.
- Pour mixture into a Pyrex (or similar) dish 350 x 250 and cook in a pre-heated oven at 175 degrees (fan assisted) for 60-70 mins.
- Pudding will still be soft when testing with a knife but will set firm when cold.

Michael Cass

THREES

This is naughty but nice and really bad for you

There are only three ingredients

Ingredients:

    3oz unsalted butter

    3oz Rice Krispies

    3 Mars bars - normal size or re arrange the weights of the other two ingredients

Method:

- Melt butter in heavy pan, add the Mars bars, chop them up it makes it easier!

DO NOT LET THE MIX COME TO THE BOIL AS IT BREAKS THE DENTURES!!

- Add the Rice Krispies and stir in well, pour into a 'swiss roll pan, or similar
- Mark into portions (fingers or squares) allow to cool and go mad!

Don't know how many it makes but they don't last long anyway!

Judi SB

AUNTY DENTY'S RECIPES

These are handed down recipes so the cups will have been teacups. Aunty Denty was born in the mid to late 19th Century.

My mum substituted the measures in the Harvo Bread by trial and error. Baking tins will probably be 1 lb bread, but it is not written down so it depends on the volume you have at the end!

Measurements are not metric, but then neither are most TOGs!

AUNTY DENTY'S HARVO BREAD

Ingredients:

- 2 cupfuls each Brown and White Flour (10 oz)
- 2 oz Lard
- 1 cupful sugar (8oz)
- 1 tsp Bicarbonate of Soda
- 1 cupful dark treacle (16oz)
- ½lb raisins
- 1½ cupfuls Milk (3/4pt)

Method:

- Mix and bake 2 hours in Moderate Oven

Editor's note – a moderate oven is: -

- Gas Mark 3 or 4
- 160/170 or 180 C
- 325 or 350 F (for those of you that haven't embraced these newfangled temps yet!)

AUNTY DENTY'S MALT BREAD

Ingredients:

- 1½ lb Self Raising Flour
- 2 large tsp Malt
- 2 large tsp Dark Treacle
- ½ tsp Bicarbonate of Soda
- ½ lb Raisins
- 2 cups Milk
- Large Pinch salt

Method:

- Melt Treacle and Malt and mix all well together.
- Mix flour, bicarb, salt together and add this and the milk (little by little) to malt and treacle.
- Bake 50 minutes in a Moderate oven (2 loaves)

Ruth Rooney

NANA'S SCRIPTURE CAKE

Ingredients:

    4 cups plain flour

    2 tsp yeast (may use baking powder instead)

    May use 4 cups of Self Raising flour instead of plain + yeast

    ½ lb butter

    2 cups sugar

    2 cups figs (or currents if you prefer)

    2 cups raisins

    1 tbsp honey

    1 cup almonds

    Spice, to taste, & a pinch of salt

    6 eggs

    1 good cup of milk or milk + water

Method:

- Beat all together and bake for 1½ to 2 hours in a Moderate oven

No record here of tin size.   I suggest 6" to 7"

Another handed down recipe – for moderate oven conversions, see Aunty Denty's Recipes – p116 / 117.

Ruth Rooney

EXCEEDINGLY FATTENING CHEESE AND POTATO PIE

As a tog, I don't do weights so just choose according to your greed level.

Ingredients:

- Mashed potato
- Diced onion
- Sliced tomatoes
- Grated strong cheddar
- Salt and pepper
- Cayenne pepper

Method:

- Microwave chopped onion. (This is my only concession to healthy cooking)
- Mix onion with mash and cheese plus salt and pepper.
- Pile into ovenproof dish
- Top with sliced tomatoes, loads more grated cheese and sprinkle with cayenne to taste.
- Bake in oven at some temperature or other until bubbly and golden.

Enjoy!

Anne Endacksi

Editor's note – in case you haven't eaten enough - we thought you might like an extra indulgence!

ESPRESSO MARTINIS

Ingredients:

- 4 fl oz espresso coffee, chilled
- 4 fl oz white Crème de Cacao
- 4 fl oz Kahlua
- 6 fl oz Vodka
- Ice

Method:

- Pour all ingredients into a cocktail shaker, (or a jug) add plenty of ice & shake/stir

- Strain into Martini glasses & serve.

Seymour Paunch

HIL'S VELVET CREAM

Ingredients:

- 1 cup fresh cream
- 1 cup condensed milk (yes really, don't panic!)
- 3 eggs
- 2 tablespoons chocolate sauce (the sort you pour over ice cream)
- 1 teaspoon vanilla essence
- ¾ to 1 cup brandy (I have also used whisky, which turns out exceptionally well also)

Method:

- Mix all above very well.

- Bottle and keep in fridge for at least 2 days and then enjoy!

(We have left it in the fridge sometimes for all of half an hour before enjoying it, and have come to no harm!)

Hilary Farell